SUPERPLONK

Malcolm Gluck writes the 'Superplonk' column in the *Weekend Guardian*. He is also wine correspondent of *City Limits* magazine and he writes a monthly wine column for the *Sunday Post* magazine in Scotland. He has also written for *Punch*, *She*, *Cosmopolitan* and the *Independent on Sunday*. He has appeared on several TV shows talking about wine, including BBC's 'Bazaar', and he has spoken about wine on BBC radio's 'Food and Drink' programme. He is a panellist on BBC radio's 'Questions of Taste' quiz show.

SUPERPLONK
Gluck's Guide to Supermarket Wine

Malcolm Gluck

faber and faber

First published in 1991
by Faber and Faber Limited
3 Queen Square London WC1N 3AU
Second edition published in 1991
This new edition first published in 1992

Photoset by Parker Typesetting Service, Leicester
Printed in England by Clays Ltd, St Ives plc

© Malcolm Gluck, 1992

Malcolm Gluck is hereby identified as author of this work in accordance
with Section 77 of the Copyright, Designs and Patents Act 1988

A CIP record for this book is available from the British Library

ISBN 0 571 16776 4

10 9 8 7 6 5 4 3 2 1

To Frank Ying,
who straightened my back
and put the idea in my head

Contents

Introduction

Well, well. There's nothing like a recession to bring everyone to their senses. And, so it seems, to bring the dead to life. The government's arch-financial executioner, Lamont in public, Lament in private, seemingly slaughtered the £1.99 bottle of wine in the 1991 budget by hiking duty to 90p. Yet it rose from the grave in spectacular fashion over the Christmas period, resurrected by the supermarkets. Its stubborn spectre continued to haunt the shelves until the April '92 budget when it received another lethal dose of increased duty and I kissed an old friend goodbye. But no. The £1.99 bottle would have none of it. Like Rasputin, it was proving impossible to finish off. The under-two-quid bottle continued to live on the shelves as a pleasant antidote to the foul-tasting medicine the recession was forcing down all our throats. It was also a reminder that raising revenue can be just as effectively achieved by reducing the cost of things as it can by increasing them, because overall sales rise.

Now, wine should be an everyday delight. Yet one government after another seems determined to punish wine drinkers as if they were indulging in a particularly uncivilized vice. Eventually, wine will become at worst a luxury, at best a mere infrequent pleasure. Yet wine is crucial to human well-being, human health and human happiness. It should be possible to buy decent wine in this country at £1.25 a bottle, and the government should reduce duty to make this possible. The increased wine consumption which would result might even bring in more government revenue than before. There is little cheer in the thought that every duty increase puts pressure on the old and the poor. Eventually they will be forced to stop drinking wine, if they haven't already. These are the people who benefit most from regular wine consumption. Those people who consider their one or two bottles a week, drunk over the weekend, to be essential to their enjoyment of life are wine drinkers to be counted, not discarded by absurd rates of duty.

Maybe we should make English red wine available on the National Health and delivered to the door of the elderly and all deserving cases on income support. We have United Dairies. Why not United Vintners? This would not only provide much-needed nourishment and cheer to deserving folk, it would also spur all those dreadful English wine growers to grub up their white vines and plant red ones.

One encouraging sign is that many supermarkets' wine sales increased spectacularly over the past eleven months. This increased business was at the expense of traditional wine merchants and uncompetitive off-licences. I take heart from this. It is increasing evidence that more and more people are finding supermarket wine to be not only of outstanding quality but also excellent value.

Yet many a so-called wine connoisseur will not be found dead buying supermarket wine. Such liquid is without individuality, it is believed, because where is the individuality in any supermarket? Seen one, seen 'em all. What's more (and worse), on whose doors do the nation's liebfraumilch and lambrusco drinkers, horror, horror, knock, if not the supermarkets'? Therefore if you want the individual touch and the individual bottle, stick to wine merchants.

What is forgotten here is that the buying skills as well as

the technical back-up now available to most supermarket chains are not bettered anywhere. Allied to this are managements at the leading supermarkets which genuinely have their own individual ways of doing things. Nothing illustrates this better than the individuals running, and working in, the wine-buying departments of the super-markets. Ten years ago Masters of Wine were a novelty in such an environment. Now these putative experts are as much a part of the supermarket scene as gondola ends.

The connoisseur will argue, of course, that the tradi-tional wine merchant provides a personal service which no supermarket can possibly match. This is true, but then this service has to be paid for and is inevitably so partial and biased that it can often be more of a disservice. 'But what happens when you take a duff bottle back?' argue the detractors. At a wine merchant you can talk over the problem. Who is there to talk anything over with at a supermarket? All I can say is that I have had no quibble from any supermarket to whom I have returned a bottle. Indeed, I have always had my money back within seconds without demur. I wish I could say the same about some of the stuck-up prats I have been forced to confront at certain wine merchants when I've returned a bottle I considered faulty.

Asda, for example, withdrew a wine from all of their stores because the product had deteriorated and was not up to standard. A *Weekend Guardian* reader brought this wine to my attention and one sip confirmed it was a faded beauty. Asda acted promptly and without fuss, with a speed I was surprised by and with a politeness I can only marvel at. I congratulate the store's chief wine buyer, Philip Clive, and I may add that many a merchant I have dealt with in the past would have had me out of the shop on my ear rather than dump a wine in such circumstances. In other areas, too, I can report that Morrisons, Safeway, Sainsbury's and Tesco have been swift, courteous, and effective in dealing with customers' problems. And they have done this in personal ways which belie the fact that these are large companies with huge turnovers.

As well as the expert buyers running supermarket wine departments, there are the expert designers who design many of the labels. I have a soft spot for label designers and an especial interest in their area of expertise. Indeed I have been twitted more than once by other wine writers about my fascination with labels. I've been told that my remit is purely the stuff in the bottle and nothing more. Yet how a wine presents itself is hugely influential, and I defy anyone, even the most profoundly gifted of wine tasters, not to be affected by a wine's livery. A good label on a good wine is a terrific combination. A good label on a poor wine merely leads to a one-off purchase. Nothing more visibly demonstrates the immense care supermarkets now take to present wine interestingly and informatively than the proliferation of attractive and sometimes startling wine labels.

Look at Asda for a start. No wine merchant ever went to such lovingly individual lengths to seduce his customers. All extreme appearances are statements of need, whether you cover your body with tattooes or your white burgundy with blue fish. Thus Asda makes its intentions clear. It wants you to *love* the store. No wine demonstrates this better than the seriously delicious Spanish red, Leon. It has as deftly beguiling a label as you could wish for. Or do I mean daftly? With Asda's label designer, the Lewis Moberly company, I'm never quite sure. This delightful uncertainty, allied to the flair of Philip Clive's wine-buying department, makes the business of doing the wine shopping at Asda less of a chore and decidedly more fun than at any wine merchant I can think of. Leon is gorgeous wine for the money and the 1985 vintage, at under £3 the bottle, rated 16 points. It is in its prime, sinuous, with beautifully developed dry, spicy fruit with a luscious hint of bitter chocolate. It slides down a treat, yet it hails from one of Spain's least glamorous wine regions. A terrific find. I cannot divine what was in the Lewis Moberley designer's mind when (s)he drew up the label but I do know what was in the grower's mind when he drew off the wine and bottled it: it was pleasure, sheer unadulterated pleasure.

There are fewer puzzles at Budgen. Pleasant own-labels are appearing more and more, it's true, and things really looked up a while back when a wine buyer with an open brief joined the store. Unfortunately this paragon, Sarah King, has since been snapped up by Safeway, and Tony Finnerty, her replacement, is only just getting to grips with things. The wines I have chosen to be included in this book are only, I hope, the start. More good things are on the way.

The Co-op has managed to hang on to dedicated marathon runner Dr Arabella Woodrow, who also finds time to run the wine department. The store's non-centralized marketing policy must madden her at times. Label design and information have improved and there seems to be a rethinking of the fatuous policy of visiting fictitious nomenclature upon every nationality's range (to wit: German wines prefaced Lohengrin, French wines Pierre Chaumont). If I had to nominate one wine to sum up the Co-op's particular style best, it would be the happily priced and quite outstanding 15-point Chilean Cabernet Sauvignon – a humdinger of a juicy, fruity wine for under £3.50.

Gateway/Somerfield has an equally no-nonsense

woman, Angela Mount, heading its wine department, and she too has a penchant for toothsome, good-value white wines from Italy, Portugal, Spain and France. Somerfield is where the wine shelves groan loudest, of course, and if the group lives up to its promise to open scores of these superstores, each showing the full range of its wine buyer's skills, a tremor of concern may register in the board-rooms of Tesco, Sainsbury's, Asda and Safeway (let alone Oddbins, Thresher and Victoria Wine). But not quite yet. Certainly, the store's entry in the £1.99 wine stakes was a worthy beast, it being the Leziria Tinto from Portugal which was an excellent summer wine, cooled and drunk with light foods.

Littlewoods isn't causing its competitors to lose any sleep at all, perhaps because most folk don't even know the store sells wine. What's more, Littlewoods' wine buyers, run by Ian Duffy, have kept a low profile this year, so the worthy wines the store does sell don't get anything like the attention they deserve from wine writers. If I had to take home just one wine from Littlewoods, it would have to be the fabulously bubbly and fatuously priced Flutelle, a sparkling wine for under £4.50 which I would happily drink in preference to many a bottle of champagne at more than three times the price.

Likely to cause more concern in competing supermarket board-rooms is Marks and Spencer with its immensely talented and enthusiastic senior wine buyer Chris Murphy, who shuffles off round the world and comes back with astounding wines like Chilean cabernet sauvignon, Australian cabernet/shiraz, Corsican chardonnay, and even cheap and terrific wine from Germany. This is the store which to a greater degree than any other achieves what every multi-retailer aspires to: only one brand on sale.

Whether you want underpants or Côtes du Rhône, St Michael's your man, and many M & S products are canonized likewise. It is interesting that this year the store departed from this policy with wine labelling when it introduced a growers' range of wines which featured the maker's names more prominently than the saint's. These wines, from Germany, the Lebanon, Italy, Spain, Australia, France and America, are innovative and, one French wine apart, outstandingly made liquids. However, it is certainly with a French wine that the store's ruthless policy of commitment to value for money is best demonstrated. This is with the declassified chablis which is forced to call itself Jeunes Vignes. This mops up 14 points without blinking and currently asks only £4.49 for the privilege of enjoying a wine better than many a so-called real chablis at twice the price. Wine buyers from several competing supermarkets have stated their willingness to swop their eye-teeth in order to have this bottle on their shelves – though whether eye-teeth represent a significant loss for a wine buyer I cannot say.

Morrisons is a newcomer to the *Superplonk* book (and my *Weekend Guardian* column) this year, purely because so many northern readers wrote and asked why it was absent. Morrisons has brought in Stuart Purdie from Peter Dominic to run their wine-buying department, and he has inherited a very sound range of wines and a senior management above him which seem, certainly on the evidence of the Morrisons' supermarkets I visited, to have 'Low Prices' running through them like 'Blackpool' through a stick of rock. Back in the spring they had their red rioja at £2.99 the bottle, and it was a Navajas production too, Navajas being a father-and-son bodega which turns out smashing wines – their 1990 walked off with 15 points with

one sip. Morrisons also offered one of the ripest of the
£1.99 bargains, the Portuguese Soveral which rates 16
points (accurately described by one of my correspondents
as tasting 'of Portuguese lorry driver's seven-day-old
socks'), yet this was not all. The store continues to have
£1.99 wines on its shelves, some of which are exceptional.
My only criticism of this excellent, fast-expanding chain
with its fifty-odd supermarkets is that it is not moving
south fast enough (or even at all). Morrisons was tradi-
tionally Yorks and Lancs, and although it's opened up in
Leicestershire, Shropshire and Lincolnshire, it would be
interesting to see how it would fare further south. This is a
purely selfish interest on my part. The Morrisons I visited
on the site of the old Sheffield cavalry barracks was not just
a superstore, it was more like a Butlins without the red-
coats. An excellent place to quieten the kids, not to mention older members of the family. It is the only
supermarket I know of with a 'Granny Attic' on the pre-
mises which sells second-hand goods on behalf of customers and charges a small commission on every sale. I very
nearly left the place with a kid's bike under my arm which
was 'in terrific nick and very little used and only eight quid
to you, squire'.

Safeway has no second-hand bikes on any of its pre-
mises, as far as I know, and no time for second-hand
thinking either. The store's wine department, run with
great humour and individual aplomb by Liz Robertson,
just gets better and better. Not only has Safeway introduced dozens of interesting new wines from all over the
world, it has also rethought its labelling policy, introduced
a great many in-store wine promotions and improved the
quality of customer information. Indeed, it has given its
wine retailing techniques a thorough spring-clean, right

down to the way the wines are displayed on the shelves. This can only add hugely to the pleasure of shopping at the store. It was already apparent that with wines like the gorgeous cabernet sauvignon from Provence, Château Richeaume 1989, Safeway had already fully committed itself to the cause of unbridled hedonism. This wine costs £7.95, rates 17 points and is sheer delight to smell, sip and swallow. It coats the teeth lovingly with dry fruit and elegant tannins and then delivers a lengthy finish of rich, sweet blackcurrant. A very individual cabernet sauvignon. But if it's cheap wine you want, along with uncomplicated drinkability, then Safeway caters for you brilliantly with its Australian shiraz. This is shipped from Oz to France, bottled and bagged, and then ferried back to Britain. Does the wine seem bruised for all this treatment? Not that I can tell. Maybe those broad Australian shoulders on the wine were built for such treatment. At £2.99 the bottle and £7.89 for the 2-litre box, a silkier, richer wine for the dosh is hard to find. The initiative in organizing the production and packaging of this wine is greatly to be applauded. This store also had its £1.99 bargains.

Sainsbury's has eight wine buyers and they've had their fair share of bargains, too. But how many in the department, I wonder, would rather like to diminish the enormous typographical possessiveness of the word 'Sainsbury's' on almost every bottle? I put this question to senior buyer Simon Blower and all he did was smile charmingly and enthusiastically show me the smart new wine labels his department has commissioned. If one wine can sum the place up, no wine does it better than Romanian Pinot Noir. A witty label, a glorious glug (going down better than ever these days) and staggering value at £2.59 – a 15-point wine of more savoury maturity than dozens of expensive red burgundies masquerading as fine wines, and a tribute to the store's negotiating skills. If imitation is the sincerest form of flattery, then this is certainly true; Sainsbury's success with this wine has led several other stores to follow in its footsteps to Romania and bring back pinot noir. The store also continues to introduce cheap wine, for the most part of excellent quality, and its grip on the loyal customer base which thrives on these bargains must be the envy of many of its competitors. The store's own-label £2.59 Minervois was bargain enough at that price, but when it was reduced to £1.99 for a short period after Christmas, it was simply incomparable – both as a keenly priced wine of true quality and as a huge incentive to shop at Sainsbury's.

Spar is an altogether different kettle of fish, and it was only through reader-pressure that I took off its lid in the last book. However, I have closed the lid on them in this edition, simply because the wine buyer of this franchised operation of small stores could not get her act together, even to the extent of sending me a wine list. I have tasted none of Spar's new wines, or new vintages of current lines, and therefore they are dropped from the book. Readers may draw their own conclusions about a store group which shows so little interest and lack of enthusiasm.

With Tesco, wine buyers are many and varied, and all very enthusiastic, so we have a number of individuals, headed by Stephen Clarke, to thank for the store's range, which is so Rabelaisian that a dedicated sot could spend eighteen months drinking and down a different Tesco bottle each day. The one wine which I would select above all others as representative of the department's style is, without doubt, the Moscatel de Valencia. It rates 15 points, costs £2.85, and is arguably the best-value dessert wine on sale anywhere. If there is any such thing as peasant pudding plonk this is it, and I love it. There is a down-to-earthness about Tesco which I enjoy. A constant striving to offer customers the best deal seems instilled into its management and staff, and a curious and very attractive bustling quality pervades the place, as if everyone had their sleeves rolled up determined to impress. I also like the way the store has concentrated on getting interesting new wines from unpromising areas. The Austrian red wine, Winzerhaus Blauer Zweigelt 1991, is a great example of this: blooming with rich, summer-pudding fruit, blooming cheerful, and blooming cheap. Easier to drink than to pronounce.

Waitrose is a curious animal. In spite of being a workers' co-operative, nowhere is there a wine department run with more individual flair. Thus Julian Brind's department has not only stocked South African wines longer than anyone else but also offers more rewarding items like the voluptuous Alsace pinot noir, the nervously elegant Vin de Savoie, and, best value of all, the fabulous merlot, Domaine des Fontaines 1991, at less than £3. But nothing demonstrates the individuality of Waitrose more eloquently than the refusal of its wine department (no doubt to the irritation of the design department which would love to make its mark on all those labels) extensively, and expensively, to employ own-labels on its wines. This adds piquantly to the flavour of shopping at the store. After all, why shouldn't supermarket wine buyers indulge their foibles, prejudices and enthusiasms just like you and me? Never forget that the thing that they buy is more volatile, more capricious, more at the mercy of God's and growers' whims than anything else a supermarket can sell. As long as no computer is created to eliminate uncertainty, and no chemist contrives to make vintages and human nature irrelevant, we'll always to able to appreciate the individuality of each supermarket's wine-buying department and the resultant individuality of many of the wines on their shelves. All that's missing is the wine connoisseur pushing his trolley. If you want to meet him, you'll find him stuffed, standing among the dinosaurs at the Natural History Museum.

Rating a wine

Each supermarket in this *Guide* is separately listed with the wines arranged by country of origin, red and white (including the very few rosés listed). *Each wine's name is as printed on its label.* The abbreviation n.v. (non-vintage) indicates that no date is given on the label.

Each wine is rated on points out of 20. This system needs explaining, first from the viewpoint of the taster and then from yours, the drinker. As a taster I rate wines 1 to 20, always putting my mouth where your pocket is.

An excellent supermarket wine can be characterized because of its price, not only because it is rewarding to drink. Take as an example Marks and Spencer's gorgeous Montepulciano d'Abruzzo. This brilliant wine rates 15 not just because it is so well made and highly drinkable but because, at under three quid, it is an astounding bargain. It would not rate as much if it cost over a tenner, and certainly not if it cost, say, £15 or £20. Though I might say that even at those prices, the wine would be far better than many wines which do cost that much.

The full scoring system, from the taster's point of view, works as follows:

20 Is outstanding and faultless in all departments: smell, taste and finish in the throat. Worth the price, even if you have to take out a second mortgage.

19 A superb wine. Almost perfect.

18 An excellent wine but lacking the depth and finesse for the top. Extremely good value.

17 An exciting, well-made wine at an affordable price.

16 Very good wine indeed. Good enough for *any* dinner party. Not expensive.

15 For the money, a great mouthful with real style.

14 The top end of everyday drinking wine. Well-made and to be seriously recommended at the price.

13 Good wine, true to its grape(s). Not great, but very drinkable.

12 Everyday drinking wine at a sensible price.

11 Drinkable, but not a wine to dwell on.

10 Average wine (at a low price), yet still a passable mouthful. Also, wines which are expensive and, though drinkable, do not justify their high price.

9 Cheap plonk. Fine for parties in dustbin-sized dispensers.

8 On the rough side. Chemicals showing through.

7 Good for pickled onions.

6 Hardly drinkable except on an icy night by a raging bonfire.

5 Wine with all its defects and mass-manufacturing methods showing.

4 Not good at any price.

3 Barely drinkable.

2 Not to be recommended to anyone, even winos.

1 Beyond the pale. Awful. Even Lucretia Borgia wouldn't serve it.

The *Guide* concerns itself largely, though not exclusively, with wines which score 10 or more points (see pages xxiii–iv for how the scoring system works from your point of view and how the *Guide* notates prices). Undoubtedly I will have missed several wines which would be worthy of mention but which now lie on supermarket shelves to blush unseen and unrated by me. This is especially true of wines the supermarkets have brought out recently but which I have been unable to taste in time. Also, you may find one or two wines included which the supermarkets have only just recently deleted. I would say, however, that this *Guide* is as up-to-date as it is humanly possible to be.

Rating System

Scoring system

Anything scoring under 10 points is to be given a wide berth. Above the magic 10, the system works like this from your viewpoint:

10,11	Nothing nasty but equally nothing worth shouting from the rooftops. Drinkable.
12,13	Above average, interestingly made. A bargain taste.
14,15,16	This is the exceptional stuff, from the very good to the brilliant.
17,18	Really great wine worthy of individual acclaim. The sort of wine you can decant and serve to ignorant snobs who'll think it famous even when it is no such thing.
19,20	Bloody marvellous. Wine which cannot be faulted, providing an experience never to be forgotten.

Prices

I cannot guarantee the price of any wine in this *Guide* for all the usual boring reasons; inflation, economic conditions overseas, the narrow margins on some supermarket wines making it difficult to maintain consistent prices for very long and, of course, the existence of those freebooters at the Exchequer who are liable to up taxes which the supermarkets cannot help but pass on to the consumer. To get around this problem, a price banding code is assigned to each wine:

Price band

A	Under £2.50	D	£5–£7	G	£13–£20
B	£2.50–£3.50	E	£7–£10	H	Over £20
C	£3.50–£5	F	£10–£13		

Although I have individually sampled every wine in this book and am solely responsible for any errors and omissions, I owe a debt of gratitude to the many people without whom I could not exist as a supermarket wine writer. My saintly spouse, Sue, must head this list, for she bears the rigours of my life with great fortitude. My very young children, Alex and Gus (often to be heard aping the appalling slurping sound I make as I taste wine) are to be thanked for never allowing me to take myself too seriously, as is my elder son, Ben. My editor, and my dear friend, at *Weekend Guardian*, Matthew Fort, is to be thanked for his continued support, as is Fiona McGill, a rare sub-editor who did not receive her training at Dewhurst's, and also Roger Alton, editor of *Weekend Guardian* itself, who always makes me feel needed. I would also like to give my Faber and Faber editors, Belinda Matthews and Sarah Gleadell (sisters in fact as well as in kind), a large hug for their unwavering enthusiasm, and to thank Emma Bagnall, Joanna Mackle and Brigid Macleod for their patience as well as all the heroes in Faber's sales and production department who do such a marvellous job. I am in Helen Dore's debt for all her correcting and subbing, and to John McConnell and Jason Godfrey at Pentagram I say 'Thank you, both' for the design of the book's cover, nothwithstanding the ridiculous person decorating it. And I would also like to record my gratitude to Diane Lamb in Sainsbury's press relations office, Viv Jawett, Marks and Spencer's press officer, Elizabeth Oldham at Safeway, and Wendy Harries Jones at Waitrose. Certain supermarket wine buyers must also be singled out for their patience with me, and I'd like to say a special thank-you to Simon Blower at Sainsbury's, Anne-Marie Bostock at Tesco, Liz Robertson at Safeway, Julian Brind at Waitrose, Chris Murphy at Marks and Spencer, Philip Clive at Asda, Stuart Purdie at Morrisons, and Angela Mount at Gateway. I must also record my debt to Fiona Lindsay and Linda Shanks for all their beavering on my behalf, and to my bank manager, Huw Young-Jones, I say thanks for looking after my overdraft so conscientiously these past years (and let's hope this is the last year). Lastly, though at times they suck every ounce of saliva from my body, I'd like to thank all the hundreds of *Guardian* correspondents who have introduced me to my new hobby of stamp and envelope collecting and licking. And to you, who bought this book, may I say thanks very much and I hope you enjoy yourself.

Asda

ARGENTINIAN WINE – *red*

Trapiche Cabernet Sauvignon Reserve 1989   13   £B
Decent spicy blackcurrant, woody and herbal.

ARGENTINIAN WINE – *white*

Trapiche Torrontes 1990   12   £B
Interesting, interesting ... well, if dry, sticky toffees and
muddy fruit interest you, that is. Curious what folk bottle
as wine. Probably at its best with mixed salad.

AUSTRALIAN WINE – *red*

**Berri Estates Cabernet Sauvignon/Shiraz
1990**   14   £C
Terrific value to spice up a beef stew (whether you drink it
or cook with it).

Hardy's Premium Red n.v.   13   £B
Excellent value.

Longleat Shiraz 1987   15   £E
A gorgeous peppered wine with depth, aromatic profundity
and a good deal of class. A gargantuan lump of leathery

rich fruit lies at the centre of the taste, surrounded by charcoal. The wine has the most gloriously off-putting label yet devised. The bottle would sit most comfortably in a herbal doctor's surgery and may well cure all manner of ills. Guaranteed to banish any blues the drinker may have.

McWilliams Hillside Shiraz/Cabernet n.v.   14   £E

McWilliams Mount Pleasant Cabernet/Merlot 1988   12   £C

Oxford Landing Cabernet/Shiraz 1988   13   £C
A little humdinger, with its spicy acidity and richness of fruit.

South Australian Cabernet Sauvignon 1988   14   £C
A big, warm bucket of fruit: figs, pears and blackcurrants. Yet curiously dry.

South Australian Shiraz 1989 (Asda)   13   £C
Tarry, earthy, rich and fruity. Very good value.

AUSTRALIAN WINE – *white*

Hunter Estate Chardonnay 1990   12   £D

McWilliams Mount Pleasant Semillon/Chardonnay n.v.   13   £C

Mitchelton Marsanne 1990   13   £C
A luscious, fruity wine with a dry edge. Very elegant.

Old Triangle Riesling, Hill Smith 1991   12   £C

Oxford Landing Chardonnay 1990   13   £C
This primly labelled beast is a most discreet and charming

wine, with none of the tigerish tinned-pineapple grip of some Aussie chardonnays.

South Australian Chardonnay 1990 (Asda)   13   £C
Salt and pepper on the fruit: makes a pleasant change.

South-East Australian Semillon/Chardonnay 1990 (Asda)   13   £B
Excellent value.

AUSTRIAN WINE – *white*

Lenz Moser Beerenauslese 1984 (half)   13   £C

BULGARIAN WINE – *red*

Merlot 1988   12   £A

CHILEAN WINE – *red*

Rowanbrook Cabernet/Merlot 1991   14   £B
Intense spicy fruit and soothing acidity.

Viña Linderos, Cabernet Sauvignon 1987   13   £C
A touch like a St-Emilion in its integrated suppleness. Very fruity (blackcurrant and raspberry) with a good finish. Good value for a wine of such mature style. Dinner-party stuff.

CHILEAN WINE – *white*

Rowanbrook Sauvignon Blanc 1991   14 £B
Staggeringly good value for money for an excellent,
refreshing, well-balanced wine. A wine specially blended
(there is some semillon along with the sauvignon blanc) for
the store, to allow it, so the wine buyer told me, to with-
stand better the long sea journey from vineyard to shelf.
This blend works very well, with even some floral fra-
grance thrown in for good measure. Rowanbrook wines
have never impressed me before this one.

Santa Helena Chilean Rosé 1991   15 £B
A lovely little plonk for the dosh. Raspberry-rich, yet drily
finished and pleasingly well-defined acidically. A rare,
appealing rosé wine which would be good with salmon
dishes.

ENGLISH WINE – *white*

Tenterden Cinque Port Classic 1989   14 £C
A pleasant, unpretentiously fruity wine of great appeal as
an aperitif. Only the silly 'Cinque Port Classic' jars. Is it
some kind of seahorse race?

FRENCH WINE – *red*

Beaujolais Villages, Domaine des Ronze
1990　　　　　　　　　　　　　　　　12　£C

Burgundy 1989 (Asda)　　　　　　　　11　£C

Cabernet Sauvignon, Domaine Bunan 1989　12　£C

Cabernet Sauvignon, Pays d'Oc n.v. (Asda)　13　£B
Rich and captivating.

Cahors n.v. (Asda)　　　　　　　　　　10　£B

Caramany, Côtes du Roussillon Villages
1990　　　　　　　　　　　　　　　　13　£B
A nondescript bouquet but thereafter some sound, soft
fruit. Good price.

Château Beauséjour, Côtes de Castillon
1988　　　　　　　　　　　　　　　　13　£C

Château de Cabriac, Corbières 1989 (magnum)
and 1990　　　　　　　　　　　　16 '89　£D
　　　　　　　　　　　　　　　　　15 '90　£B
This wine, the '90 vintage excepted, continues to amaze for
the money. The big bottle makes the experience even more
wonderful and the terrific '86 and '88 vintages have been
followed up by an '89 which has a greater, more complex
bouquet and structure. Easily one of the best bargains on
any supermarket shelf with its haunting aroma of berries,
leaves and gently charred wood, deep, rich flavour (always
rather austere with this wine but outstanding with roast
food) and firm finish. The 1990, available in single-bottle
size, is also delicious, and improving all the time.

Château de Parenchère 1989   12 £C

Château du Bois de la Garde, Côtes du Rhône n.v.   13 £C

Château Hanteillan 1988   13 £D
Classy assemblage here – good bouquet, firm body, excellent fruit.

Château Haut-Saric 1990   13 £B
This wine is exclusive to the store and the '89 vintage was superb. This follow-on vintage isn't quite so gripping.

Château Mayne de Grissac 1989   13 £C

Château Thibaut 1989   12 £B

Château Val-Joanis, Côtes du Luberon 1989 and 1990   12 £C

Châteauneuf-du-Pape, Château Fines Riches n.v.   12 £D

Claret n.v. (Asda)   12 £B

Côtes du Duras n.v. (Asda)   12 £A

Domaine de Barjac 1990   12 £B

Domaine de Grangeneuve, Coteaux du Tricastin n.v.   13 £C

Domaine de St-Laurent 1991   13 £B

Domaine Haut Galine 1990   12 £B

Fleurie, Clos de la Chapelle des Bois 1990   14 £E
With my sniffy attitude to modern beaujolais, I rarely find examples in supermarkets I can muster one whit of enthusiasm for. I can muster several whits for this one.

Fronton, Côtes Frontonnais 1989 (Asda)   11   £B
Previous vintages of this wine were highly rated, but it
seems to be becoming too austere.

Merlot d'Oc n.v. (Asda)   13   £B
Old socks to smell, but ignore this, for the fruit is very
properly dressed and agreeably welcoming.

Morgon, Michel Jambon 1990   13   £D
Not as hammy a wine as you might think.

Moulin-à-Vent, Château des Jacques 1988   11   £E

Organic Claret, Château Vieux Georget 1988   12   £C

Red Burgundy 1989 (Asda)   11   £C

Santenay, Foulot, Château Perruchot 1988   12   £E

St-Chinian n.v. (Asda)   13   £B
Light and fruity and good value.

St-Emilion n.v. (Asda)   13   £C
This supple blend of merlot and cabernet franc is a typical
St-Emilion, making it an attractive luncheon wine.

**Syrah, Vin de Pays des Collines Rhondaniennes
n.v.**   14   £C
An engaging mouthful of tobaccoey fruit and chewiness.

**Vin de Pays des Bouches du Rhône n.v.
(Asda)**   12   £B

Vin de Pays des Côtes de Gascogne n.v.   12   £C

Volnay, Domaine Henri Boillot 1986   13   £F

FRENCH WINE – *white*

Blanc de Blancs n.v. (Asda)	11	£B

Burgundy 1990 (Asda)   11   £C

Cabernet de Saumur, Rosé n.v.   13   £B
Good value, good fruit, good style.

Chablis 1989 (Asda)   12   £D

Chablis Grand Cru Bougros 1988   12   £G

Chablis Premier Cru 1988 Fourchaume   13   £E
Gorgeous wine with the delicate, balanced finesse of fruit
and acidity that is typical of first-rate chablis. The bouquet
is lightly toasted, with a touch of lemon, with sesame seeds,
appearing in the taste. It is only a mite disappointing in the
finish which, perhaps inevitably, cannot quite live up to the
beginning. Lovely stuff, but expensive.

Chardonnay, Pays d'Oc n.v. (Asda)   12   £B
Good standard plonking.

Château Filhot 1985   15   £D
Not a bad price considering the trouble to which
humankind is put in order to make this dessert wine from
mouldy grapes (which require expert picking, for a start).
This example is a fine wine, splendid for the Christmas
pud, with its lovely touches of honeyed fruit.

Château Fondarzac, Entre-Deux-Mers 1991   13   £C
Great with shellfish.

Château Laville-Bertrou 1991   12   £C

Château Mouney 1989   11   £C

Chenin de l'Aude 1990   14 £B
An excellently balanced wine of some character. Great
value. Very modern in style, clean and fresh. Don't go near
muscadet when you can pick up quality like this at so much
less.

Domaine de la Tuilerie 1991   14 £C
Wonderfully shaped fruit, fructose-finished, reminiscent
of pears and damsons. Good balance. Rich, and subtly
unctuous, the wine has a lovely feel.

Domaine de St-Laurent 1991   13 £B
Good level of fruit, rather dusty aroma, but good value for
large gatherings.

Gewürztraminer 1990 (Asda)   12 £C

Mâcon-Vire, Domaine des Chazelles 1989   12 £D

Muscat, Cuvée Henry Peyrottes n.v.   15 £B
Marvellous individual dessert wine for almost any pud. A
touch of grilled molasses under the blowsy toffeed honey
gives it great presence in the mouth. Miraculous value for
money.

Muscat de Beaumes de Venise n.v.   14 £D
It strikes me that Beaumes de Venise has become so
consistent in its style and unchanging in what it delivers to
the drinker, particularly as an accompaniment to fresh soft
fruits, that it seems as if every bottle emanates from the
same maker. This one is no exception. Standard gorgeous
drinking.

Pinot Blanc 1989 (Asda)   12 £C

Rully, Domaine du Chapitre 1987   11 £E

Sancerre, Château de Thauvenay 1990   12 £D

Vin de Pays des Côtes de Gascogne n.v.   13   £C
The usual banana-and-peach aroma and taste, but nicely
controlled in this example. Happy rustic hooch and a
happy rustic price.

GERMAN WINE – *white*

Baden Dry n.v. (Asda)   12   £B
A German with a sense of humour? Not quite, but certainly an uncharacteristic German; dry and unfussily fruity
and excellent with shellfish.

Bereich Bernkastel n.v. (Asda)   11   £B

Herxheimer Honigsack Beerenauslese n.v.   12   £E

Mainzer Domherr 1988 (Asda)   13   £B

Niersteiner Rosenberg, Metternich 1989   11   £C

Niersteiner Spiegelberg 1990 (Asda)   11   £B

Rudesheimer Rosengarten n.v. (Asda)   11   £B

Wachenheimer Rechbachel 1988   12   £D
Sherbert-lemon dog's teeth nipping at your taste-buds. A
Billy Cotton of a wine: *Wakey! Wakey!*

Wehlener Sonnenuhr 1990   12   £D

Wiltinger Scharzberg 1989   11   £B

HUNGARIAN WINE – *red*

Cabernet Sauvignon, Villany 1991	12	£A

Merlot, Villany 1991 — 13 £A
Excellent value – soft, rubbery, fruity.

HUNGARIAN WINE – *white*

Gyongyos Estate Sauvignon Blanc 1991 — 15 £B
This is great stuff at a great price. (See under Safeway for more details.)

Muscat, Dunavar 1991 — 12 £A

Pinot Blanc, Dunavar 1991 — 10 £A

ITALIAN WINE – *red*

Bardolino (Asda) — 12 £B

Chianti 1990 (Asda) — 13 £B
Also available in magnums, this wine is excellent value: a soft, plummy, very attractive proposition for all pasta dishes.

Chianti Classico 1989 (Asda) — 12 £C

Ciro, Librandi 1988 — 14 £C
Maturely fruity and gorgeously teeth-gripping, like a fruit cake with fangs. Terrific with Italian food.

Montepulciano d'Abruzzo, Miglianico 1990   13   £B

Rosso di Montalcino, Val di Suga 1989   14   £C
These wines always remind me of trim, terracotta versions
of those hairy Australian wines which are all tar and ripe
figs. This wine is reminiscent of those things, but with an
elegance and an aplomb and a perfect weight of fruit. It has
softness and sweet melon ripeness and offers bitter almond
on the finish.

ITALIAN WINE – *white*

Bianco di Custoza 1989   13   £C
Delicious, but perilously close to a fiver.

Chardonnay di Alto Adige n.v. (Asda)   14   £C
Well-made chardonnay with a clean finish. Nicely unfussy
yet fruity, it can be agreeably drunk on its own or with
food.

Est! Est!! Est!!! 1990   13   £C
Lovely soft, melony fruit with a grapey acidity. Smashing
aperitif. Ridiculous name, of course, but that all adds to the
fun. (And I do know why the wine is so-called, so any
would-be correspondents – of which there were many
when I last expressed a view as to the wine's silly moniker –
please down your pens!)

Frascati n.v. (Asda)   11   £B

Lugana, Santa Christina 1989   14   £D
If the price of white burgundy is giving you a headache
(like the wine itself can), then chuck your hard-earned
dosh at this instead. Delicate, subtly flowery and clean but

thoroughly Northern Italian in manner: a fine Latin/
Alpine mix in both style and flavour. A splendid wine.

Orvieto Classico, Cardeto 1990	12	£B

Pinot Grigio, Ca Donino 1990   12   £C

Verdicchio delle Marche n.v. (Asda)   13   £B
Excellent soft fruit and clean acidity. Good value and great
with fish.

LEBANESE WINE – *red*

Château Musar 1982 and 1983   16 '82   £D
                                     17 '83   £D

A lovely balance of body, depth and quite volatile spiciness.
A distinguished wine with mature, oaky character under
the fruit. The '83 is an exceptional year.

NEW ZEALAND WINE – *white*

Delegat's Sauvignon Blanc 1990   12   £D

PORTUGUESE WINE – *red*

Dão 1987   14   £B
A handsome bundle of attractive baked fruit. It cries out,
or rather melodiously bawls, for food. Quite outstanding
value.

Douro 1988 (Asda)   13   £B
Ripe, well-muscled, impressively fruity – and easier to
swallow than Schwarzenegger. Good with rich foods and
cheeses.

PORTUGUESE WINE – *white*

Douro n.v. (Asda)   13   £B
Excellent value for dinner parties. Goes especially well
with chicken in cream sauce.

Vinho Verde n.v.   13   £B
It is difficult to fault this 9 per cent-alcohol, petticoat-
pretty wine with its edgy lemon fruit and great slug of
acidity. A good palate-tickler.

ROMANIAN WINE – *red*

Feteasca Cabernet Sauvignon n.v.   10   £B

Romanian Pinot Noir 1986   14   £B
An approachable wine of freshness and fruit, belying its
middle age, and terrific value for money.

SOUTH AFRICAN WINE – *red*

Clearsprings Cape n.v.   13   £B
Can't argue with the value-for-money aspect of this wine.

Landskroom Pinotage 1990   10   £C

SOUTH AFRICAN WINE – *white*

Clearsprings Cape n.v.   13   £B
Dry, but with lots of ripe melon and plummy fruit and a
rather sweet fruit finish. Good price.

Danie de Wet Rhine Riesling Reserve 1991   15   £C
Easily the most toothsome vinous confection from the
Land of the Great Divide yet to pass my lips. Fabulous,
stylish lush fruit with superb, searing acidity. A great aperitif (and at 8 per cent a light one) or to accompany hard fruit
and pastry desserts.

Van Louveren Chardonnay 1990   12   £D

Van Louveren Sauvignon Blanc 1991   13   £C
A wine so young and sprightly in character it's like a child
in nappies learning to crawl.

SPANISH WINE – *red*

Don Darias n.v.   12   £B

Leon 1985 and 1986   16   £B
Sinuous, with beautifully developed dry, spicy fruit, with a
hint of chocolate, the '85 slips down a treat and is one of
the under-three-quid bargains of our times. Hasn't a harsh
note anywhere. Many drinkers will think of it as some
marvellous oddity from South America or the northern

Rhône rather than as a bumpkin from one of Spain's least glamorous wine regions. The '86 is not as developed as the '85.

Montecillo 'Viña Monty', Rioja 1985   10   £D
Amusing aroma of stale cabbage and prunes (if prunes do smell of anything – I rather fancy they do). After this heroic start, it falls off somewhat, rather like an Adonis on a spring-board doing a belly-flop rather than executing a perfect dive.

Navarra n.v. (Asda)   13   £B
Rat-tails' smell but marvellous fruit.

Penedes n.v. (Asda)   14   £B
Oh joy! Beef stew finds its perfect partner after advertising for decades. Dry, with figgy, bitter fruit, this wine is a cheap smasher.

Rioja 1987 (Asda)   13   £C

Torres Corõnas 1986   14   £C
Made by one of Spain's master magicians. He throws grapes into vats and they conjure themselves into velvet fruit bowls.

Valencia Red n.v.   11   £B
The label sports a condom with a green hat on. It's certainly trying to tell us something, but for the life of me I cannot figure out what.

Vega Cubillas, Ribero del Duero 1986   13   £C

Viña Albali, Valdepeñas 1986   13   £B

SPANISH WINE – *white*

La Mancha 1990 (Asda)   14   £A
Outstanding, complex even (just a touch): fruity, dry and
clean, and terrific value for money.

Moscatel de Valencia n.v.   15   £B
One of the best-value pud plonks on the planet.

Valencia Dry n.v. (Asda)   13   £A
Great value. Clean, citric, bright with fruit.

USA WINE – *red*

Colombia Pinot Noir 1987   15   £D
Under seven quid, this has to be one of the most impressive pinot noirs on sale. Its major competition of the same
1987 vintage is not from Burgundy but from Oregon and
California. Woody, gamey, scrumptious fruit held in check
by the characteristic vegetal pinot noir framing, it is a
bargain wine for serious pinot freaks. This wine makes me
wish my nearest Asda was round the corner. The '88
vintage, coming up, I have yet to taste.

Sebastiani Pinot Noir n.v. (magnum)   13   £E
A most agreeable wine in a most agreeable big bottle, ideal
for a dinner or lunch for four or five people.

USA WINE – *white*

Sebastiani Chardonnay n.v. (magnum)	13	£E

Sebastiani Dry White Zinfandel 1990	13	£C

A rosé by any other name is still a rosé, and this is a rosé in spite of being called white. This should not spoil your enjoyment.

SPARKLING WINE/CHAMPAGNE

Australian Pinot Noir/Chardonnay n.v.	14	£D

Delicious introduction to the fruit as your nose enters the glass, and then come lots of melon and pear-drop fruit which are not cloying but nicely packaged acidically so that the wine has good balance. Good value.

Ayala Château d'Ay 1985	10	£G
Cava n.v. (Asda)	12	£C
Champagne Brut n.v. (Asda)	12	£F
Champagne Rosé Brut n.v. (Asda)	14	£F
Crémant de Bourgogne 1987 (Asda)	13	£D

Why bother with the pretentions of Rheims when Burgundy makes this fine little sparkler?

Edmond Mazure Australian Brut 1989	12	£D

Budgen

AUSTRALIAN WINE – *red*

| Jacob's Creek Dry Red n.v. | 12 | £B |

Penfolds Bin 389 Cabernet/Shiraz 1988   13   £D
Velvet figs.

South-East Australian Shiraz n.v.
(Riverina/Budgen)   13   £B
This really is bargain drinking.

AUSTRALIAN WINE – *white*

South-East Australian Semillon n.v.
(Riverina/Budgen)   12   £B

AUSTRIAN WINE – *white*

Winzerhaus Grüner Veltliner 1991   14   £C
Under £4, this is a terrific bargain. See under Tesco for
more details.

CHILEAN WINE – *red*

Underraga Pinot Noir 1989   11   £B
Intense strawberry-and-cherry aroma fronts a wine which
disappoints in the bleakness of its fruit after such a promising start.

FRENCH WINE – *red*

Château de Malijay, Côtes du Rhône 1990   13   £C

Côtes du Rhône Villages n.v.   13   £C

Delas Crozes-Hermitage n.v.   10   £C

Domaine Luth, Côtes du Vivarais 1991   13   £B
Rich , plummy bargain.

Faugères, Jean Jean n.v.   11   £A

Le Haut Colombier, Vin de Pays de la Drôme
1991   14   £B
Lovely, soft little thing. A bargain black cherry taste.

Madiran, Domaine de Fitère 1987   12   £C
Good cheap claret type.

Vin de Pays des Coteaux de l'Ardèche 1990   12   £B
You need a beak as long as the woodcock on the label to
catch the bouquet, but thereafter the wine's drinkable
enough. Good value for large numbers of drunks.

FRENCH WINE – *white*

Blanc de Blancs Cuvée Spéciale n.v.	10	£B

Chablis, Domaine St-Marc 1988	10	£D

**Chardonnay, Domaine les Terres Blanches
1989** 13 £C
Eric and Chris – nice one.

Château Fondarzac 1991	13	£B

**Château Le Gordonne, Côtes de Provence Rosé
n.v.** 13 £C
Pleasant summer rosé (dry) with strawberry bubble-gum
aftertaste.

Corbières, Blanc de Blancs 1990 13 £B
Outright bargain. Not as determinedly keen-edged as it
might be, but attractively fruity all the same in a quiet way.

Gewürztraminer, Gisselbrecht 1989 14 £C
Expensive but lovely. Spicy lychee fruit plus clean acidity.

**Le Bonnefois, Vin de Pays des Côtes de Gascogne
n.v.** 13 £B
Bargain.

Listel, Blanc de Blancs Sur Lie 1990	12	£B

Listel, Domaine de Bosquet-Canet 1989	11	£C

Listel, Domaine de Villeroy-Castellas 1991	13	£B

Muscadet Sur Lie, Beauregard 1989	11	£B

Pinot Blanc, Gisselbrecht n.v.	12	£C

Sancerre, Les Grandes Dames 1989   11   £D
As like a true sancerre as a pair of my socks. Unlike my
socks, however, the wine is not woolly and disagreeably
smelly, but merely pleasantly plonkish without the chic one
is entitled to find in a wine costing this money calling itself
sancerre.

Tuilerie du Bosc, Côtes de Mont 1990   13   £B
Softened in oak, yet with the firm freshness of youth – a
pleasant wine all round.

GERMAN WINE – *white*

Bereich Bernkastel 1991   8   £B

Longuicher Probstberg Kabinett 1989   10   £C

Wachenheimer Domblick Kabinett 1990   12   £B

HUNGARIAN WINE – *red*

Cabernet Sauvignon n.v.   13   £B

Merlot n.v.   11   £B

HUNGARIAN WINE – *white*

Chardonnay n.v.   8   £B
Comes from the Gyongyos vineyard, but without the

Ryman touch, and the absence is sorely missed. (See under Safeway, Sainsbury *et al.* for more on the subject.)

Sauvignon Blanc n.v.	8 £B

ITALIAN WINE – *red*

Barolo, Cortese 1987   13 £C
Rich liquorice, cherries and blackcurrant – and a little spice. Yet soft. A fancy slurp.

Chianti Classico, Castelgreve 1989   11 £C

ITALIAN WINE – *white*

Lugana, Villa Flora 1989   14 £C
The best white wine in the whole store? Certainly the Zenato family, who make this wine, rarely seem to put a foot wrong as they stamp out one elegant wine after another on Lake Garda's shores. This one is beautifully clean and fresh, yet the fruit is sheer citric velvet.

NEW ZEALAND WINE – *red*

Montana Cabernet Sauvignon 1990   12 £C

NEW ZEALAND WINE – *white*

Villa Maria Sauvignon Blanc 1991   14 £C
Like a fruitier sancerre. Really quite distinguished
drinking.

PORTUGUESE WINE – *red*

Dão, Dom Ferraz n.v.   13 £B
Great sausage-and-chips wine.

PORTUGUESE WINE – *white*

Vinho Verde n.v.   6 £B
Smells like someone urinated into the glass. Tastes mar-
ginally better.

SOUTH AFRICAN WINE – *red*

Table Mountain 1991   14 £B
An excellent, thorough-going bargain. Tastes exactly like
Waitrose's Far Enough 1991 (see page 192).

SPANISH WINE – *red*

Castenada n.v. (1 litre)   12   £B
A bargain wine for lots of people and mountains of pasta.

Don Carvi Navarra n.v.   13   £B

Viña Albali 1986   14   £B
Creamy vanilla aroma, rich vanillaey fruit plus a good finish. Mature as it is, it'll probably improve in bottle for a couple more years.

SPARKLING WINE/CHAMPAGNE

Lindauer, New Zealand n.v.   13   £D
Good fizzer.

Paul Cheneau Cava n.v.   6   £D
'Famous the world over for its elegant style and subtle aromas' says the label on the back. In every respect, this is the reverse of the truth. You would get more body and fruit from a glass of Perrier water with a handful of sugar added.

Co-op

AUSTRALIAN WINE – *red*

Cabernet Sauvignon, Berri n.v.   13   £C
Terrific with roast turkey stuffed with dried fruits.

Shiraz n.v.   14   £C
Minty, tarry, fruity – good New World style. Very good value.

AUSTRALIAN WINE – *white*

**Columbard and Chardonnay, Cranswick
n.v.**   12   £C

Semillon n.v.   12   £C

BULGARIAN WINE – *red*

Cabernet Sauvignon n.v.   11   £B

BULGARIAN WINE – *white*

Welchriesling and Misket n.v.   12   £B

CHILEAN WINE – *red*

**Cabernet Sauvignon, Viña Santa Helena n.v.
(Co-op)**   15   £B
The new batch of this wine rates three points higher than
the old. For, in spite of the ugly, unwelcoming bottle (the
awful label gives the least prepossessing of health shop
tonic wines a good run for its money), this is a really
handsome, welcoming wine. It hums with warm, fruity
flavours and soft tannins and is superb with grilled
chicken.

CHILEAN WINE – *white*

Sauvignon Blanc, Curico Valley n.v.   13   £B

ENGLISH WINE – *white*

English Table Wine, Three Choirs n.v.   11   £C

FRENCH WINE – *red*

Anjou Rouge n.v.   12   £B
This wine is made from an undervalued grape called
cabernet franc which is not to be confused with the famous

cabernet sauvignon. This franc devaluation is to the wine-drinker's advantage, for it makes very interesting and good-value wine in the Anjou area of France, in particular Bourgueil and Chinon. This Anjou is not in their class but nevertheless it has some of the rustic charm of its most illustrious cousins; this is especially in evidence in the bouquet, which has the distinct hint of lead pencils. The taste, however, is not as unappetizing as it sounds, being fruity, dry and reasonably rounded. Anjou rouge can be drunk chilled, like beaujolais.

Bergerac Rouge 13 £B

Bergerac first found fame with the eponymous Cyrano, but his length of nose is unnecessary with so forward a bouquet as this wine exhibits. A country plonk, yes, but with a mite more character and backbone than many, and this is reflected in the rating. It also has an agreeably fruity finish; unlike some rural simpletons, it does not imagine its job is over once you have swilled it around the mouth. Good with roasts and hearty dinners, it has, nevertheless, enough going for it to be drunk on its own.

Charles Vienot, Côtes de Beaune Villages
n.v. 12 £D

Château Cissac 1982 and 1984 '82 12 £E
'84 11 £E

Château du Piras n.v. 14 £C

A proper structure to this wine gives it a typical petit-bordeaux style, with its fruitiness held firmly in check by an attractive, dry edge. It also has an immediate matey quality, unlike so many bordeaux with their stiff-mannered approach demanding years of ageing and hours of breathing before they agree to embrace you as a drinking companion.

Châteauneuf-du-Pape, Cellier des Princes 1989	11	£E

Claret n.v.	12	£B

Corbières n.v.	11	£B

Coteaux du Tricastin n.v.	12	£B

This wine comes from a pleasant French town called Valréas, where Rhône bargains are often to be unearthed. This is a simple, gulpable, fruity yet dry wine with no mean characteristics whatsoever. It cannot set the universe ablaze, but it would agreeably set off sausages and mash with a healthy dollop of mustard.

Côtes de Provence Rouge n.v.	12	£B

Côtes du Rhône n.v.	11	£B

Côtes du Roussillon n.v.	11	£A

Côtes du Ventoux n.v.	11	£B

Fitou n.v.	12	£B

Mâcon Rouge n.v.	12	£C

Médoc n.v.	12	£C

Vin de Pays de l'Aude n.v.	11	£A

Vin de Table Red n.v.	11	£A

FRENCH WINE – *white*

Alsace Gewürztraminer n.v.	11	£C

Alsace Pinot Blanc n.v.	13	£B
Alsace Riesling n.v.	10	£B
Anjou Blanc n.v.	13	£B
Bergerac Blanc n.v.	11	£B
Blanc de Blancs n.v.	11	£B
Bordeaux Blanc Medium Dry n.v.	12	£B
Bourgogne Blanc n.v.	10	£D

Chablis, Gustave Devilaine 1989   11   £E
This wine would be better at £3.25. It's not got the elegance you've a right to expect at nigh on nine quid.

Côtes de Provence Rosé n.v.	10	£B
Gallière, Sauternes 1988	11	£E
Premières Côtes de Bordeaux n.v.	11	£B

Rosé d'Anjou n.v.   12   £A
A goodish, firm little rosé.

Sauvignon Blanc n.v.   11   £B

Vin de Pays de la Vallée du Paradis, Grenache n.v.   13   £B

Vin de Pays d'Oc, Sauvignon Blanc n.v.   13   £B

Vin de Pays des Côtes Catalanes n.v. (magnum)   13   £A
A very good wine for this sort of money. Fruity and not without some style.

Vin de Pays des Côtes de Gascogne n.v.   12   £B

Vin de Pays des Côtes des Pyrénées Orientales
n.v.   13   £B

GERMAN WINE – *white*

Bereich Nierstein n.v.	12	£A
Bernkasteler Kurfustlay n.v.	12	£A
Deidesheimer Hofstuck Kabinett 1988	13	£B
Hock Deutscher Tafelwein n.v.	11	£A
Klusserather St-Michael n.v.	13	£A
Liebfraumilch n.v. (Co-op)	10	£A
Mosel Deutscher Tafelwein n.v.	11	£A
Moseltaler n.v.	11	£B
Niersteiner Gutes Domtal n.v.	13	£A
Oppenheimer Krotenbrunnen n.v.	11	£A
Piesporter Michelsberg n.v.	12	£B
Rudesheimer Rosengarten n.v.	12	£A

Urziger Schwarzlay Spätlese n.v.   12   £C
The wine's flowery fruitiness and acidity make it what most
people will characterize as sweet. It is well made and has
some charm but it has insufficient flesh to go with main-
course food and its fruitiness is too puny to tackle desserts.

Zeller Schwarze Katz n.v.   10   £B

ITALIAN WINE – *red*

Barolo, Roche 1984	11	£D

Chianti 1990	10	£B

Merlot, Vino da Tavola del Veneto n.v.   13   £B
Soft on the pocket, soft on the palate. A good light wine
with gracious manners. Lacks muscle, but that is the style,
so drink it with salads and hors d'oeuvres.

Otto Santi, Chianti Classico 1987   13   £D
Big woody aroma reminiscent of a rioja, but with just
enough of its grape variety's (sangiovese) tannin to give it
that subtle bitterness bequeathed to the Tuscan by virtue
of climate, sun and soil.

Valpolicella n.v.   12   £A

ITALIAN WINE – *white*

Bianco di Custoza n.v.   12   £C
Pretty label, pretty wine (light, gentle, daisy-fresh), but a
mite too close to four quid for comfort.

Frascati n.v.	10	£B

Orvieto Secco n.v.   12   £C
Typical orvieto with its acidic, citric finish. This hints at a
certain zestiness in the wine which is best with fish.

Soave n.v.	10	£A

Verdicchio Classico n.v.	12	£C

PORTUGUESE WINE – *red*

Bairrada 1987	14	£B

PORTUGUESE WINE – *white*

Bairrada 1989	12	£B
Dão 1988	13	£B
Portuguese Rosé n.v.	10	£B
Vinho Verde n.v.	11	£B

SPANISH WINE – *red*

Gran Condol, Rioja Reserva 1984   13   £D
The creamy, vanilla quality of this wine can be quite
objectionable in some circumstances, like overlipsticked
lips, but in this case the effect is lovely. One of the few red
wines I can imagine wrestling with chicken tikka and living
to tell the tale.

SPANISH WINE – *white*

Dry White n.v.	10	£A
Medium White n.v.	10	£B

YUGOSLAVIAN WINE – *red*

Merlot n.v. (Co-op) 13 £B

Yugoslavian Merlot n.v. (Co-op) 14 £B
Excellent value. Good, soft, glugging plonk with true
varietal character.

SPARKLING WINE/CHAMPAGNE

Cava n.v. 11 £C

De Clairveaux Brut Champagne n.v. 13 £F
Yeasty and fruity.

De Clairveaux Rosé Champagne n.v. 12 £G
If you must drink such things, this is as reasonable a wine
as any other at the price, but that price is high.

Sekt n.v. 11 £B

Sparkling Liebfraumilch n.v. 10 £C

Sparkling Liebfraumilch 1989 9 £C
Interesting year for this wine.

Sparkling Saumur n.v. 13 £C
Good, firm fruit and acidic presence.

Gateway/Somerfield

AUSTRALIAN WINE – *red*

Australian Grenache Shiraz n.v. (Somerfield)	14	£B

Outstanding value – dry yet fruity, faintly spicy.

Berri Estates, Barossa Valley Cabernet Sauvignon 1987	14	£C

How many things can you spend a fiver on which instantly fill your head with sunshine?

Corbans Merlot/Cabernet Sauvignon 1989	14	£E

Handsome twinning of the Bordeaux grapes provides deep, fruity drinking.

Grenache/Shiraz, Hardy's n.v. (Somerfield)	12	£B

Seaview Cabernet/Shiraz 1989	14	£C

De-de-delicious.

Seaview Sauvignon 1989	13	£C

AUSTRALIAN WINE – *white*

Australian Dry White 1991 (Somerfield)	14	£B

Dry? At a pinch. The deep-plum-and-berry fruit gives it a bright roundness, however, which is tasty. Delicious, all the same.

McLaren Vale Oaked Chardonnay 1991	13	£C
Penfold's Chardonnay 1990	12	£E
Penfold's Padthaway Chardonnay 1990	11	£E

AUSTRIAN WINE – *white*

Winzerhaus Grünerveltliner 1991   **14** **£C**
Whistle-clean acidity, good fruit. An excellent wine for the money.

CHILEAN WINE – *red*

Chilean Cabernet Sauvignon 1990   **13** **£B**
Great-value friendly cabernet drinking.

CHILEAN WINE – *white*

Peteroa Sauvignon Blanc 1991   **13** **£B**

CHINESE WINE – *white*

Tsingtao Chinese Chardonnay n.v.   **12** **£C**
(See Sainsbury's.) Basically this is a typical Australian chardonnay. At £4.99 it's expensive. Perhaps too expensive. But it's worth 12 points and bags of curiosity value.

FRENCH WINE – *red*

Beaujolais 1990 (Somerfield)	10	£C
Beaune 1988	12	£E
Bergerac 1990 (Somerfield)	13	£B
Bourgogne Pinot Noir 1988	12	£C
Brouilly 1991	12	£C

Château Barbe-Blanche 1987   14   £D
A supple, rather drier than normal St-Emilion offering easy drinking and fruity approachability at a reasonable price.

Château Citran 1987   13   £E
Bordeaux's worst label but very far from being the region's worst wine. Dry, woody, toasty fruit with a luxuriant elegance.

Château de Caraguilhes 1989   15   £B
Wine notes June 1991: big, brawny organic stuff. Keep for a year and it'll be even better (13 points). Wine notes May 1992: outstanding now the wine has matured to perfection. (It's actually, I've just realized, the wine in my hand on the front cover.)

Château de Quilhanet 1989	13	£A
Château la Menardie 1989	13	£C
Château la Rocheraie 1989	10	£C

Château la Terrasse, Côtes de Castillon n.v.   13   £C
A mature bordeaux, typically tannic, but showing no graceless hardness. Very good value.

Château St-Justin, Côtes du Rhône 1989   13   £C
Another Lancon production of a possible declassified
Châteauneuf-du-Pape contender. Grenache, cinsault,
mourvèdre and syrah make a handsome if not perfectly
integrated bunch – the result is a fruity wine of bite and
depth.

Château St-Robert, Graves 1987   13   £C
Nice style, nice price. Dry and fruity with a distant hint of
the cedarwood aroma of fine Graves.

Château Talence 1989   13   £C

Châteauneuf-du-Pape, La Jacquinotte 1988   13   £C
This is tough, chewy but very attractive – due, I think, to
the mourvèdre grape variety's inclusion in the blend. It is a
full wine, not immediately fruity but very approachable if
you don't mind the absence of the softness this wine
normally demonstrates. Good with roast foods.

Chinon, Pierre Chainier 1989   12   £C

Claret n.v. (Somerfield)   13   £B
Cheap way to enhance the roast lamb.

Côtes de Gascogne n.v.   12   £A

Côtes de Roussillon Villages 1989   12   £B
Nice touch of stalky richness.

Côtes du Marmandais 1990   12   £B
Marmande grows terrific tomatoes, and perhaps this
accounts for the interesting tomato-fruit dimension to the
stalky dryness of this wine.

Domaine de Bonserine, Côte-Rotie 1989   10   £G

Domaine de la Solitude, Côtes du Rhône 1991   11   £C

Domaine des Couteaux des Travers 1990 13 £C

Domaine Fontarney 1979 14 £D
I've had bottles of this particular wine maturing in my
coal-hole since 1983. It was awful then – it needed to
unbung its closed bouquet and release its fruit. Now it's
ready and Gateway have it at a reasonable price (it is after
all the second wine of Château Brane-Catenac, third-
growth St-Estèphe, and is made by one of Bordeaux's
most impressive wine-makers, André Lurton). The fruit is
still restrained, austere almost, but it's an elegant though
stiffly mannered wine with a distinguished claret feel. Very
good with dinner-party roasts.

La Solitude, Châteauneuf-du-Pape 1989 15 £E
Black cherry cake and acid. A lovely, tasty, aromatic wine
of beguiling softness and satiny drinkability.

Marsannay 1989 13 £D

Médoc n.v. 11 £B

Merlot, Domaine de la Magdelaine 1991 13 £C

Minervois, Jean Jean n.v. 12 £A

Red Burgundy 1990 (Somerfield) 12 £C

Santenay 1988 12 £E

St-Chinian 1990 13 £B

St-Joseph 1989 15 £D
A deeply sustaining broth of herbs and vegetables and rich,
rich fruit. Yumsville.

Vacqueyras, Vieux Clocher 1990 14 £C
Dry earth, damsons and black cherries. A smashing little
Rhône beauty.

FRENCH WINE – *white*

Bordeaux Sauvignon 1990 (Somerfield)   12   £B

Chablis 1990 (Somerfield)   13   £D

Chais Baumière Chardonnay 1990   13   £C
What do Australians get up to in the South of France?
Drink this and find out that they make themselves at home.

Chardonnay, Vin de Pays de l'Hérault 1991   14   £C
Good touch of bright, clear fruit. A good, well-made
specimen.

Château Bastor-Lamontagne 1989 (half)   14   £D
A useful half-bottle at a less than useful price, but this is a
gorgeous pudding wine.

Château de Montredon 1991   14   £B
Altogether nicely put together and terrific value.

Château du Chayne 1991   12   £C

Château du Queyret 1990   13   £B

Domaine de Marignan 1991   14   £B
Good full fruit, clean, dry finish. Excellent value for richer
fish dishes and chicken.

Domaine des Garbes 1990   13   £C
Excellent value for a pudding wine of this style.

Hautes Côtes de Beaune 1989   12   £D
Pleasant touch of gaminess on the soft fruitiness. White
burgundy at a reasonable price.

Meursault, Jaffelin 1990   13   £G
The real thing: musty, green and rich – concentrated cat's
pee and ripe melon, no less.

Montagny Premier Cru 1989   12   £D

Sancerre, Les Chanvières 1990   12   £D

White Burgundy 1990 (Somerfield)   13   £C
Toast on the nose, a little butter on the fruit. A good
breakfast burgundy.

**Vin de Pays des Coteaux de l'Ardèche Blanc
n.v.**   13   £B
Terrific value. Very clean. Good with shellfish.

GERMAN WINE – *red*

Dornfelder 1990   13   £C
Plummy, ripe, high-pitched – the perfect public school
red.

GERMAN WINE – *white*

Baden Dry n.v.   13   £B

Niersteiner Spiegelberg 1991   12   £B

Oberemmeler Rosenberg Riesling 1989   11   £D

Oestricher Doosberg Riesling 1983   14   £C
A riesling coming up for its tenth birthday at this price is a
bargain and demonstrates to those who say they dislike

German wines that, with a few years under their label, they can be superb. This wine's tartaric acidity, the dominant characteristic of the riesling grape, is on great form here and would, I bet, fall in love with the equally distinctive acidity of asparagus to the extent that they could well produce that rare perfection of a heavenly marriage.

Rheinpfalz Riesling Trocken 1988	12	£C
St-Johanner Abtei 1988	12	£B
St-Ursula Weinkellerei Bingen Morio Muskat n.v.	11	£A
St-Ursula Weinkellerei Bingen Pinot Blanc Trocken Gallerei Range n.v.	11	£B
St-Ursula Weinkellerei Bingen Rheingau Riesling n.v.	11	£B
Trocken n.v. (Somerfield)	13	£B

An excellent salad wine. (Salad with lots of tasty bits in it.)

HUNGARIAN WINE – *red*

Bull's Blood n.v.	13	£B

HUNGARIAN WINE – *white*

Gyongyos Estate, Dry Muscat 1991	15	£B

Lovely light, melony aperitif wine, with subtle muscat undertones, which is outstanding value for money.

ITALIAN WINE – *red*

Barolo, Castiglione Faletto 1986 12 £D
A chewy, chocolate-biscuit rich wine. Excellent with pungent foods.

Cabernet Sauvignon del Veneto 1991 11 £B

Chianti, Conti Serristori 1989 13 £B
Go for its dry earthy fruitiness, curranty richness and almost ripe dryness. For a vast bowl of garlicky pasta and lots of friends around the table, the wine is superb.

Copertino 1990 14 £B
Excellent value for money for utterly simple, dry, fruity wine-drinking which is incomparably unpretentious and satisfying.

Merlot, Grave del Friuli 1991 11 £B

Montereale 1990 14 £B
Rubber and old flower-pots. Zingy cherry acid. Great value and a great wine for pastas.

Riserva di Fizzano, Chianti Classico 1986 14 £E
Elegant, rich, mature. Superb companion for a cold evening.

Rubizzo 1991 13 £C

ITALIAN WINE – *white*

Caldeo 1990 13 £B
Lemons and raspberries – a subtle fruit salad set off by a

dash of Venetian acidity. Delicious value for money.

**Chardonnay del Piemonte 1990, Viticoltori
dell Acquese**   13   £B
A very fresh chardonnay with the fruit cutting a dash rather
than the acidity. Great with fish and chicken.

**Frascati, Principe Pallavicini 1991
(Somerfield)**   12   £C

Montereale 1990   13   £B
You can't grumble at the price, bitch about the pleasant
fruitiness, or complain about the streak of fresh acidity.
But *I* can grumble at yet another decent white wine at
Gateway (this one is Sicilian) which gives me a headache
trying to find a fresh way to describe it.

Pinot Bianco del Veneto 1990   12   £B

Pinot Grigio del Veneto 1991   12   £B

Prunalbo 1990   11   £C

Terre di Ginestra 1990   13   £C
For a fuller description of this wine see under Tesco.

LEBANESE WINE – *red*

Château Musar 1983   17   £D
This is the wine which was once the greatest wine made
under fire for under a fiver in the world. Thankfully the
fire has gone, but regrettably so has the fiver. However, the
wine is still outstandingly mature drinking with its volatile,
woody, roasted fruitiness, great length and superb, deep-
hearted generosity of feeling.

PORTUGUESE WINE – *red*

Dão, Reserva 1987   14   £B
Oooh . . . lashings of lovely baked fruit at a give-away price.

Leziria n.v.   14   £B
A bargain, perfectly weighted alcoholically, which may be drunk, chilled or otherwise, when cheap young luncheon beaujolais or valpolicella is unavailable. The interesting addition of some pinot noir to the traditional periquita grape variety has softened the fizziness of this grape (which always likes to breathe for an hour before it is gulleted) and has added an attractive cherry, edgily nutty quality to the ripeness.

PORTUGUESE WINE – *white*

Bairrada 1990   13   £B

Bairrada Branco 1991   15   £B
Gorgeous, well-organized wine: ripe fruit, keen acid. Brilliant value for money for grilled fish and chicken.

SOUTH AFRICAN WINE – *red*

Cape Selection Pinotage 1991   13   £B
Good value.

SOUTH AFRICAN WINE – *white*

Chenin Blanc 1991   13   £B
This is strictly for rice and fish dishes.

SPANISH WINE – *red*

Don Hugo n.v.   14   £B
Great bargain boozing for spicy sausages and curries.

Raimat Tempranillo 1988   16   £D
One of Western civilization's greatest food-wines.
Wonderful pungent, classy, rich fruit which is quite superb
with chicken and chorizo stew. It was born to be drunk with
olive oil and garlic and, though I have no scientific evidence
for it, I have a notion that this wine adds twenty years to the
lifespan of anyone who drinks merely a bottle a month.

Sēnorio de Agos, Rioja Reserva 1985   13   £D
Mature and ripe; not over the hill but definitely over food.

Sēnorio de Val 1988   15   £B
What a ridiculous price! Beautiful vanilla, coconut and
banana woodiness and lengthy blackcurrant fruit. For all
that, a dry wine and quite delicious.

Viña Albali 1981   13   £C
Cloying, toffee-nosed fruit of considerable maturity, and a
great support for all manner of edible things, like grilled or
roasted vegetables drenched in olive oil, garlic and herbs, or
spicy kebabs, or even a pizza.

Viña Albali Riserva 1984   14   £B
It's creamy, vanilla-ey, blackcurranty and rather forceful.
Drink with equally characterful dishes.

SPANISH WINE – *white*

Don Hugo Blanco n.v.   13   £B
Vanilla-and-coconut fruit and grapefruity acidity. Great
with a fish curry.

Penedes Blanco 1990   13   £B
Very attractive balance of fruit and acid.

Rioja Blanco 1988   12   £C

Rioja Blanco Mariscol 1988   13   £C

Somontano Montesierra 1990   13   £B
Outstanding little chardonnay-type wine. Excellent value –
delicious fruitiness, plummy and citric, allied to tongue-
tingling cleanness.

Valencia Dry White n.v.   13   £B
Outstanding value for money. Dry, fruity, simple and
gluggable.

USA WINE – *red*

Glen Ellen Cabernet Sauvignon 1988   12   £C

Sebastiani Zinfandel 1988   11   £C

USA WINE – *white*

Sebastiani Chardonnay 1990   12   £C

SPARKLING WINE/CHAMPAGNE

Cava, Conde de Caralt n.v. (Somerfield)   15   £C
One of the best-value sparklers for under a fiver in Britain.
Terrific wine that puts many a champagne to shame.

Chardonnay Santi Vino Spumante Brut n.v.   13   £C
Excellent aperitif sparkler.

Crémant de Bourgogne, Cave de Lugny n.v.   12   £D
Excellent structure. Good balance. Very good value.

Moscato Fizz n.v.   13   £A
Not strictly wine at 4.75 per cent alcohol. Under two quid
a bottle, though, so who's going to bitch? Terrific stuff for
teenage parties with lots of ice-cream.

Prince William Blanc de Blancs   14   £G
Nigh on fourteen quid is a lot for a bottle of wine, but this
is a classically brut champagne and is better in style than
some *grandes marques* with fancy reserve titles costing a lot
more.

Prince William Brut Reserve n.v.   13   £F

Prince William Brut Rosé n.v.   13   £G
This is one of the better rosés, if you must touch the stuff.

Raimat Chardonnay Brut n.v. 14 £D

Can't afford mature vintage champagne? Fear not. Stick your nose in a glass of this and then swig and forget Rheims ever existed.

Vouvray, Tête de Cuvée n.v. 14 £D

Knock-out champagne sub.

Wiltinger Sharzberg Riesling 1987 13 £C

Great for summer garden parties with its bubbly peachiness.

Littlewoods

AUSTRALIAN WINE – *red*

Jacob's Creek Dry Red n.v.   13   £C
Full-bodied but not too overdeveloped – complementary
to carnivores' favourites like steak and onions.

Windsor Ridge Shiraz n.v.   12   £B
Pleasing touch of mint on the fruit.

AUSTRALIAN WINE – *white*

Jacob's Creek Medium Dry White n.v.   11   £B

Windsor Ridge Semillon n.v.   13   £B
Excellent with spicy chicken dishes.

BULGARIAN WINE – *red*

Bulgarian Cabernet Sauvignon n.v.   12   £B

FRENCH WINE – *red*

Château d'Aigueville 1989   13   £C
Country wine at a bargain price: fruity, dry, rounded with

agreeably complete structure. The sort of bottle which is typical of the sunny Rhône in its suggestion of burliness under the fruitiness.

Côtes du Rhône n.v. (25 cl)	10	£A
Merlot de Caumont n.v.	10	£B
Vin de Table Red n.v. (Littlewoods)	12	£A

FRENCH WINE – *white*

Côtes du Rhône (25 cl)	4	£A
Rosé d'Anjou n.v. (Littlewoods)	13	£A
Vin de Table Dry n.v. (Littlewoods)	10	£A
Vin de Table Medium n.v. (Littlewoods)	10	£A

GERMAN WINE – *white*

| Hock n.v. | 11 | £A |

Morio Muskat n.v. 13 £A
A simple aperitif of remarkable acidic/fruit balance. Outstanding value for money.

| Moselle n.v. | 11 | £A |

St-Johanner Abtei Auslese n.v. 12 £C
A glass is fine before a meal, or, with a mild tart or hard fruit, after one.

HUNGARIAN WINE – *red*

Cabernet Sauvignon n.v.	12	£A

Merlot n.v. 14 £B
The Villany region's merlot seems to be one of the best bargains of any wine list on which it appears. A great, soft-hearted pasta wine.

HUNGARIAN WINE – *white*

Chardonnay n.v. 8 £B
Ugh!

Gewürztraminer n.v. 10 £B
This stuff is actually getting better. A while ago I wouldn't have wished a glass on my worst enemy.

Olasz Riesling n.v. 12 £B

Sauvignon Blanc n.v. 12 £B

ITALIAN WINE – *red*

Chianti II Borgo n.v. 10 £B

Valpolicella n.v. 10 £B

ITALIAN WINE – *white*

Frascati n.v.   12   £B
A good aperitif wine.

Soave n.v.   12   £B

PORTUGUESE WINE – *red*

Bairrada n.v.   13   £B
Very good value – a curranty, rich wine lending great
distinction to any dish.

Dão n.v.   14   £B
This has all the typical characteristics of a well-made Dão.
Chocolatey, fruity yet dry, and excellent value for money.

ROMANIAN WINE – *red*

Romanian Cellars Merlot/Cabernet n.v.   12   £B

Romanian Pinot Noir 1986   14   £B
Bargain. Mature, composty, dry, fully assertive fruit. A
distinguished Central European with courtly manners.

ROMANIAN WINE – *white*

Romanian Cellars Riesling/Muscat n.v.
(magnum)   12   £D
Dog-fur smell but a pleasant, fruity aperitif tipple for all
that.

SPANISH WINE – *red*

Rioja, Tondeluña 1989   13   £C

An excellent-value-for-money rioja. Well made.

SPARKLING WINE/CHAMPAGNE

Asti Martini n.v.   10   £D
Terribly sweet young thing.

Estrella n.v.   10   £B

Flutelle n.v.   14   £C
This wine is so impressive for the money that one smart
bride-to-be I invited to try it announced, after the third
glass, that she would insist on it being served at the recep-
tion instead of champagne, thereby saving a fortune.

Kupferberg Gold n.v.   10   £D

Monsigny Champagne n.v. (Littlewoods)   11   £F
Solid rather than exciting.

Marks and Spencer

AUSTRALIAN WINE – *red*

Cabernet/Shiraz n.v.   15   £C

An astonishing, creamy roquefort cheese and menthol
aroma which is surprisingly enticing. Then comes rich
gamey fruit cut with acidity as bracing as a sea breeze. The
finish lingers beautifully. I knocked up a cayenne pepper
and green cardamom fried chicken and vegetable dish to
test my theory that this wine would be great with such
subtle, spicy food, and I was rewarded with a marvellous
supper.

Riverina Nouvelle n.v.   14   £B

Wonderful striking nose of cherries and ginger; joyous,
keen fruit. The only tasteless thing about it is the label.

AUSTRALIAN WINE – *white*

Len Evans Chardonnay 1991   15   £D

Exuberant with fruit, yet not overboiled or offputtingly
teeth-embracing; truly long and bright and, dare I say it, a
touch elegant and refined? It's dry in the final analysis and
one of the few Aussie chardonnays it is possible to imagine
accompanying a good book rather than a good bonk.

Riverina Nouvelle n.v.   12   £B

New-mown grass, hay and pear-drops.

Semillon/Chardonnay n.v.   12   £C

BULGARIAN WINE – *red*

Cabernet Sauvignon, Svischtov Region 1988   13   £B
Earth-and-grass smell, dry but sweet-finishing cherry-
and-plum fruit which doesn't carry quite through to the
finish.

Country Red n.v.   12   £B
Old apples, pears and cabbage water.

BULGARIAN WINE – *white*

Bulgarian Country White n.v.   12   £B

CHILEAN WINE – *red*

Cabernet Sauvignon n.v.   15   £C
Christmas dinner: don't serve the gravy, just serve this
wine. It smells of minty Ribena, then delivers a punchy
mouthful of soft, satiny fruit reminiscent of blackcurrant,
and then back comes the mint on the finish. A gorgeous
wine to have with well-hung grouse.

CHILEAN WINE – *white*

Chilean Sauvignon Blanc 1991	11	£B

FRENCH WINE – *red*

Beaujolais 1990	12	£C
Beaujolais Villages, Georges Duboeuf 1991	13	£C
Bouches du Rhône n.v.	10	£A
Bourgogne, Epineuil 1989	13	£D

This is an interesting wine. The appellation is a neglected one, only recently enjoying a revival (thirty years ago only one grower made the stuff). Made by the La Chablisienne co-op which turns out such terrific chablis for M & S, this is a burgundy which will, I reckon, get better and better. Certainly this '89 vintage is one up on the '88.

Brouilly 1990	12	£D
Cabernet Sauvignon n.v.	11	£B
Châteauneuf-du-Pape, Les Couvesets 1989	13	£E
Claret AC n.v. (1 litre)	14	£C

Excellent value. Decant it and it will surprise the neighbours when you have them in for a simple supper.

Comte Tolosan 1991	13	£B
Côtes de St-Mont 1989	13	£C

Côtes du Rhône n.v. (1 litre)   14 £C
Firm, fruity; a lovely southern mouthful.

Domaine de l'Orangerie n.v.   13 £B
Very dry, with good brambly fruit, and very good value.

Fitou 1989   11 £B

Fleurie 1990   12 £E

French Country n.v.   14 £B
One of the easiest and softest-drinking country wines
around, and one of M & S's best bargains.

Full Red Côtes du Roussillon n.v. (1 litre)   12 £B

Gamay n.v.   12 £B

Margaux, Château Notton 1988   13 £E
The only thing that's not on with this wine is the price-tag:
not because it's nigh on a tenner but because in order to
enjoy the wine at its most sublime you'll have to put that
tenner away in a cool dark place for some years.

Médoc, Château de Medalli 1989   13 £C

Merlot, Christian Moueix 1989   14 £C
Spicy grassiness on the fruit, which finishes supply and
smoothly, makes this a classic merlot of some distinction
and, for the money, not bad value, since it suggests a
pedigree bordeaux in feel despite its solo grape variety.

Selection Rouge, George Duboeuf n.v.   13 £B
Mulled clove aroma, tastes of plums and soft berries with a
touch of pepper. Bit of a wimpish finish and personality by
itself, but with food it's much better.

St-Emilion, Château Gros Caillou 1990   14   £D
Lovely supple wine of winning warmth.

St-Julien, Léoville-Barton 1984   13   £E

FRENCH WINE – *white*

Blush, Frizzante n.v.   12   £B
Fruity charm complemented by its pretty colour, marred
only by its awful name which sounds like the *nom de danse*
of the least talented of a Folies Bergères line-up.

Bouches du Rhône n.v.   11   £A

Burgundy, Caves de Lugny 1989   12   £C

Chablis 1990   14   £D
Lovely classic, flinty stuff.

Chablis Premier Cru Beauroy 1988   16   £E
This is a very expensive white wine, but if you want to
experience what a beautifully structured, pedigree beast
chardonnay can be, then this chablis is it. It is superb in its
fruity greenness yet restrained, elegant richness, and better
than many a raddled meursault at loads more money.

Chardonnay, Cellier des Samsons n.v.   14   £C
This has a typical farmyardy chardonnay pong and an
uncomplicated, fruity taste. Very good value.

Chardonnay de Chardonnay 1990   14   £C
Coming from the village near Mâcon which gives the grape
its name, this wine is a standard-bearer and, like Man-
chester United in another context, it does not disappoint. It

certainly finishes better than United. The fruit is beautifully framed by the acidity and the whole effect is refined drinkability.

Côtes de Gascogne 1990   13   £B

Very good value – dry, freshly fruity (not tinned) and harmoniously acidic.

Cuvée du Chapelain n.v.   14   £B

This wine travels brilliantly. The grapes, from the airen variety which carpets Spain, cross the Pyrenees into France to be made into an excellent little wine by Claude Houbart. From a most sneerworthy grape Houbart squeezes every ounce of aroma and flavour. The combination of melon-freshness in the mouth with a finish of peach and banana is excellent, subtle, very appealing.

Domaine Samuletto 1990   15   £C

A chardonnay from Corsica – a much depreciated vineyard surrounded by sea which is beginning to produce interesting wines. This example is remarkable for the money. It introduces itself with aromas of melon and gooseberry with an edge of sweated vegetables, the hallmark of good chardonnay, then carries this fruit theme to the mouth and finishes freshly. A wine with true pretensions to elegance.

French Country n.v.   13   £B

Fresh, with firm fruit, this is excellent value and great with shellfish dishes.

French Dry White Anjou n.v.(1 litre)   13   £C

Good value and good clean fun. A happy blend of chenin and sauvignon grape varieties. Ideal for lots of people at a fish supper.

French Medium White n.v. (1 litre)	12	£B

Jeunes Vignes n.v.	14	£C

Several supermarket wine buyers would give their eye-teeth to have this lovely chablis-in-all-but-name on their shelves. Tremendously posh drinking for under a fiver.

Les Trois Collines 1991	13	£B

Sour melon fruit and plenty of friendly acidity. This is a bargain.

Mâcon Villages 1990	12	£D
Pinot Gris 1990	12	£C
Pouilly Fumé 1990	12	£D
Rosé d'Anjou n.v. (1 litre)	12	£C
Sancerre, La Charmette 1990	12	£D
Sauvignon n.v.	11	£B
Selection Blanc, George Duboeuf n.v.	12	£B

GERMAN WINE – *white*

Bereich Nierstein 1991	11	£B
Herbert Koch Rheinhessen n.v.	12	£B
Hock n.v. (1 litre)	11	£B
Jurgen Bibinger Rheinpfalz n.v.	13	£B
Liebfraumilch n.v.	10	£B

Moselle n.v. (1 litre)   11   £C

Piesporter Michelsberg 1990   12   £C

Roland Sander Dexheimer Doktor 1991   15   £B
This richly endowed, dryish wine has great aromatic
attractions. The scheurebe grape amongst the ubiquitous
müller-thurgau (from which so much dull English wine is
made) gives the wine considerable presence in the mouth,
along with a level of keen finishing elegance surprising for
so little money. A great aperitif and excellent with light
soups and mixed salads.

ITALIAN WINE – *red*

Barbera d'Asti 1990   14   £B
Good value for such refined yet beefy slurping. A roast
beef Italian rather than a spag bol merchant. Has attractive
rounded fruit to the dry edge and an expensive feel all
round.

Barolo 1987   13   £D
A demure, well-mannered, smooth barolo with little evidence of the liquorice, figs, and all those rich, acrid things
this sort of wine normally abounds in.

Chianti Classico, Villa Cafaggio 1988   13   £D
Delizioso, squisito, gustoso.

Italian Table Wine n.v. (1 litre)   10   £B

Lungarotti Cabernet Sauvignon 1987   14   £C
Smooth, very, very dry blackcurrant with a woody edge to
it. Rather good with chicken and duck dishes, and possibly

game, although I suspect it'll improve even more over the next couple of years. I am totally uninfluenced in liking this wine, you must believe, by the fact that it is made by an extremely personable woman; in a country with a greater percentage of male chauvinist pigs than an English gentlemen's club at throwing-out time, Teresa Lungarotti's feat is considerable.

Montepulciano d'Abruzzo 1990 15 £B
Soft gulpability at an astoundingly easy-to-swallow price. Joyous, bold, life-enhancing, this hugely fruity wine is just great with pastas and sausages, tomato salads, jugged hare, and life in general ... my wife says it even makes dinner with a balding, fattish old fart like her husband bearable.

ITALIAN WINE – *white*

Bianco Veronese 1991 13 £B
Great value for such firm, clean, fruity drinking.

Chardonnay n.v. 14 £C
A well-structured wine with pretensions to class even at this price. Dry yet firmly fruity, with that typical Italian chardonnay 'bite', it is very good value for money.

Frascati Superiore 1990 13 £C
Pleasant, clean wine with a touch of fruit.

Italian Table Wine n.v. (1 litre) 11 £B
This label speaks true; a solid and versatile party wine.

Orvieto Superiore 1990 11 £B

Soave n.v. (1 litre) 10 £C

LEBANESE WINE – *red*

Hochar 1989   **15 £D**
This is the easiest-to-drink wine Château Musar has ever
produced. Named, says Serge Hochar, after his new
grandchild, this is an appropriately youthful wine, without
the usual five years' ageing, and the blend is restricted to
cinsault and cabernet sauvignon. So there is no volatility
from the usual grenache and syrah; just an effortlessly
bright and smooth, fruity wine of great length and flavour
(loganberries and blackberries), but the whole effect is
what is so captivating – it is truly wonderfully slip-
downable yet, at the same time, is distinctly Musar. A
lovely young thing and a lovely young price.

PORTUGUESE WINE – *white*

Vinho Verde n.v.   **13 £B**
I'm a fan of this wine. Light green by name, green by
nature, unfussy, supple, very light. Very good aperitif.

SOUTH AFRICAN WINE – *red*

Cape Country Pinotage 1989   **12 £B**
Leathery, boxy, some ripe fruit.

SOUTH AFRICAN WINE – *white*

Cape Country Chenin Blanc 1991   13   £B
Bright apple and melon. Very pleasant stuff.

Cape Country Colombard 1991   11   £B

Cape Country Sauvignon Blanc 1991   14   £B
There really is some style here for just over three quid.
Indeed, there are sancerres on sale at twice the price which
are only half as good. Grapefruit, gooseberry, citrus –
they're all there and nicely balanced.

Cape Nouveau 1992   12   £B
Refreshing liquorice and fruit-gum flavour.

Chenin Blanc 1991   13   £B
The bouquet of spicy grass and flowers is attractive. One
of the less overboiled South Africans.

Colombard 1991   12   £B
Good value. Good weight of fruit.

SPANISH WINE – *red*

Rioja   13   £B
Good price for a well-made rioja with assertive fruit but
not the bullying variety.

Marqués de Grinon, Rueda 1990   15   £D
What a powerful argument this wine is for the superiority
of the gifted individual over the massed, ponderously
stupid ranks of the bureaucrats. For years the Marqués

watered his vines, flying in the face of the regulations, but his cussed persistence created excellent products, and the regulations, in the end, changed. His wine possesses a glorious fruit/acid balance which makes it hard to believe it hails from near Toledo (unless you consider the steely edge to the fruit is due to the proximity of the grapes to the city which once produced the keenest swords in Europe), and the lovely subtle, flowery undertones produce a thirst-quenching elegance.

USA WINE – *red*

Napa Valley, California 'N' n.v.   14   £C
A sprightly, youthful wine skilfully blended from gamay (giving it freshness and fruit) and petit syrah (providing subtle spiciness and body).

USA WINE – *white*

Woodbridge, Robert Mondari Chardonnay 1989   14   £D
There is spice to this peach of a wine, but also freshness and fullness.

SPARKLING WINE/CHAMPAGNE

Blanc de Blancs Champagne n.v.   12   £G

Blanc de Noirs n.v. 15 £F

A champagne of great depth and style. Superb with food due to its dry yet fruity elegance being beautifully held by a pastry crust of flavour.

Cava n.v. 12 £C

A typical yeasty cava. Might go down well with a shellfish stew.

Champagne, Veuve de Medts n.v. 14 £G

This is a gorgeous experience, even one for which you have had to shell out nearly £14 (the same price as one of Marks's natty cotton shirts). Elegant, full yet dry, with a soothing acidity typical of champagne at its incomparable best.

Crémant d'Alsace n.v. 14 £D

Fool the champagne snobs with this one. Through aroma, taste and finish in the throat, an excellent little fizzer.

Crémant de Bourgogne n.v. 12/13 £D

Desroches n.v. 13 £F

Also very usefully made in misanthropic half-bottles.

Hérard Champagne n.v. 13 £F

Nicholas Feuillatté 1982 14 £G

Quite something to find a gorgeous near-ten-year-old champagne reclining cheek-by-jowl with a check-out counter at my local M & S. Can it be that even the receipt of a mere penny change out of £20 does not dispirit the store's notoriously well-heeled impulse buyers?

Saumar Ladubay 1989 15 £D

What a little corker! A gorgeous chenin/chardonnay blend of quite arrogant aplomb.

Sparkling Chardonnay n.v.   13   £D

Sparkling Medium Dry n.v.   12   £C

Sparkling Monmousseau 1988   14   £D
A first-class champagne substitute. Firm, not over fruity,
dry – good value.

Sparkling Rosé n.v.   14   £C
Superb little fizzer – lively, floral, fruity all the way
through, yet nicely acidic. A bargain.

St-Gall 1985   12   £G
Vintage champagne at this price should be all of a piece –
aroma, body, flavour and sparkle, all moving together in
those tiny bubbles. This one, whilst rich and very drinkable, seems to overplay itself somewhat and have a discon-
certingly incongruous fatness of taste. At its best with
smoked salmon with lemon and black pepper.

Morrisons

ARGENTINIAN WINE – *red*

Trapiche Malbec 1988   14 £C
Made 100 per cent from a grape variety which forms
between 5 per cent and 10 per cent of many Bordeaux
wines, this oddity from South America is excellently structured and primly fruity. Very dry and at its best with
well-sauced roasts.

AUSTRALIAN WINE – *red*

Coldridge Shiraz/Cabernet Sauvignon 1989   14 £B
The touch of burnt sweet honey to the lovely rich fruit,
never cloying, is very attractive. Good balance – trips very
nicely on and off the tongue.

Wood Duck Dam Cabernet Sauvignon n.v.   14 £B
Dirt cheap for seriously well-made cabernet which would
go extremely well with the duck on the label (the sort of
ridiculous-looking beast that deserves a thorough
roasting).

AUSTRALIAN WINE – *white*

Cascades Estate Chardonnay n.v.   16 £B
It is difficult to think of a classier chardonnay for under £3
than this. It really is a most happily balanced, firmly fruity
wine of vegetally classic undertones and refined acidity.

Coldridge Estate Late-Picked Muscat 1991   13 £B
A bargain aperitif for connoisseurs of such tipples.
Engaging immediately with spicy fruit, the wine then
delivers a subtle thrust of acid, and with its sweet-edged
finish, a healthy come-on to the taste-buds.

Coldridge Semillon/Chardonnay n.v.   15 £B
Fantastic value for a great touch of buttery fruit, clean
acidity and terrific style.

Koonunga Hill Semillon/Chardonnay 1991   13 £C
Forward, sunny and as subtle as a tiger shark.

Wood Duck Dam Semillon n.v.   12 £B
Like its red partner, this is a duck wine – this one might do
well with the plum-sauced Peking variety.

CHILEAN WINE – *red*

Gato Negro Cabernet Sauvignon 1989   12 £B

San Pedro Merlot 1989   14 £C
Dark, rich, with well-developed fruit. A fine roast-meat wine.

Valdezaro Cabernet Sauvignon n.v.   14 £B
Very good value. A marvellous sausage-and-mash wine.

CHILEAN WINE – *white*

Chilean Sauvignon Blanc n.v.	13	£B
Gato Blanco Sauvignon Blanc 1991	12	£B

FRENCH WINE – *red*

Cellier la Chouf, Minervois n.v.   14   £A
Excellent-value, softly tannic, friendly wine.

Château Cantenac, Côtes de Bourg 1988   13   £C
A far from indecent bit of claret at a very decent price.

Château Font du Loup 1989   14   £C
Superb value for an excellent, handsomely austere and po-faced minor bordeaux which will improve over the next two years.

Côtes du Rhône 1990 (Morrisons)   12   £B
Light but very drinkable.

Côtes du Rhône, Louis Bonnard 1991   10   £A

Fortant Cabernet Sauvignon n.v.   12   £B

Fronton 1989   14   £C
This is about as old as the negrette grape variety can get, it seems, before it becomes senile. This wine totters a bit but it is excellent with food and, if you like the taste you get from chewing coal, prunes and blackcurrants, plus that pert dryness, then you've got yourself a great bargain packaged in an absurd painted bottle like an illustration from *The Water Babies*.

La Rose St-Jean, Bordeaux n.v. (half)   14   £A
A simple light claret of great interest to solo lunchers.
Good touch of soft fruit on the woodiness.

La Vieille Ferme, Côtes du Ventoux n.v.   12   £B

Vin de Pays Catalan n.v.   12   £A
Nice touch of cherry fruit.

Vin de Pays Coteaux de l'Ardèche n.v.   13   £A

Vin de Pays de l'Ardèche n.v.   10   £A

Vin de Pays des Pyrénées Orientales n.v.   15   £A
Fantastic value for loads of raspberry and blackcurrant
fruit lightly packed in a gentle acidity.

FRENCH WINE – *white*

Cépage Muscat 1990   13   £B

Colbois Petit Chablis n.v.   11   £C

Côtes de Thau 1991   14   £B
Lots of nice clean fruit plus lots of everything else except a
big price-tag.

Côtes du Rhône n.v.   12   £B

Jalibert Bergerac Sec n.v.   10   £B

Pinot Blanc, Victor Preiss n.v.   13   £C
Good fruit, keen balance, a typical well-made Alsatian.

Vin de Pays de l'Ardèche n.v.   12   £B
Not a mass of fruit but agreeably flinty. Good with fish.

GERMAN WINE – *white*

| Herxheimer Herrlich Kabinett n.v. | 13 | £B |

| Klusserather St Michael 1991 | 10 | £B |

Oppenheimer Sacktrager Riesling Kabinett n.v. 14 £C
Louis Guntrum turns out splendid wines of great finesse, sharply defined fruitiness and good acidic balance. A classic riesling aperitif.

Shellfish Dry 1990 13 £A
This is really quite decently made up to the finish. But at the price the wine lives up to its name well – i.e. very good with shellfish.

| Wiltinger Scharzberg Spätlese 1989 | 13 | £B |

GREEK WINE – *red*

Mavrodaphne of Patras n.v. 10 £B
This is basically stewed prunes made into wine. Probably rather good with Christmas pudding.

HUNGARIAN WINE – *white*

Gewürztraminer n.v. 2 £B
Well, the label's on straight.

ITALIAN WINE – *red*

Gabbia d'Oro n.v.   8   £A
This has the virtue, admittedly, of being under £2, but it is
also under just about everything else, including any decent
amount of fruit.

Montepulciano d'Abruzzo n.v.   13   £B
Good value. Dry, yet cherryish and cheering.

Sangiovese di Romagna n.v.   13   £B

Valpolicella (Morrisons)   12   £B

ITALIAN WINE – *white*

Del Colle Chardonnay n.v.   13   £B

Frascati Superiore n.v. (Morrisons)   12   £B

Orvieto Classico, Bigi 1990   13   £C
Nicely made. Good firm fruit and a clean finish.

Trebbiano del Veneto 1990   11   £B

MEXICAN WINE – *white*

L. A. Cetto Chenin Blanc 1989   12   £C
A curious little number with a talcum-powder quality to
the fruit. (Though it is not recommended you try
sprinkling the wine over yourself after a bath.)

PORTUGUESE WINE – *red*

Borges Bairrada 1987   14   £B
Just the right amount of bottle-ageing to give the rich, ripe fruit a nicely dusty character. Terrific value for Christmas stuffed fowl.

Soveral n.v.   16   £A
Great plummy acidity and dry cherry and blackcurrant fruit. A typical ripe wine from the Land of Port – one which needs an hour's breathing to get over its journey before being drunk. Fantastic value.

PORTUGUESE WINE – *white*

Portuguese Rosé n.v.   12   £B

Vinho Verde n.v.   12   £B

ROMANIAN WINE – *white*

Sauvignon Blanc 1990   14   £B
A dry, properly made sauvignon blanc with clear, clean character, above-average style and determined class. Excellent value.

SOUTH AFRICAN WINE – *white*

Cape Country Chenin Blanc 1990   14   £B
Face powder, white peaches, wood – an interesting recipe
for an attractive wine which is fruity, refreshing and good
value.

SPANISH WINE – *red*

El Morano Carineña 1987   13   £C
Sweet-finishing with mature fruit and a good depth of
flavour. Interesting.

Rioja 1990 (Morrisons)   15   £C
Excellent value for excellently balanced wine of dry, subtle
charms (the vanilla touches from the oak-ageing are
neither strident nor misplaced) and attractive fruitiness.
Made by the Navajas family, who really do seem to turn out
the vinous equivalent of a hand-made product.

SPANISH WINE – *white*

Portalet n.v.   10   £B

Spanish Dry n.v. (Morrisons)   13   £A
Great value for large groups.

SPARKLING WINE/CHAMPAGNE

Asti Spumante n.v. 10 £C
A small glass with banana cake might do.

Moscato Spumante n.v. 11 £B
Shaving-foam in a glass.

Nicole d'Aurigny Champagne n.v. 16 £E
One of the darkest-hued and most satisfying champagnes I have ever drunk. A stunner for the dosh. Were I to be hanged in the morn, and solicitous of my hangman's pocket, this would be the champagne I would choose.

Schloss Bochingen n.v. 10 £C

Seaview Brut n.v. 15 £C
One of the best-value sparklers on the market – stylish, refined, and quite delicious.

Vouvray n.v. (Morrisons) 14 £D
Good-value sparkler.

Safeway

AUSTRALIAN WINE – *red*

Jacob's Creek Dry Red 1989	13	£C
Jamiesons Run 1989 (half)	11	£C
Orlando RF Cabernet Sauvignon 1987	13	£C

Penfold's Bin 222, Eden Valley Cabernet Sauvignon 1985   14   £E
Keep your teeth sharp to bite into this chewy number.

Penfold's Bin 28 Kalimna Shiraz 1987	13	£C

Penfold's Bin No. 2 Shiraz/Mataro 1989   15   £C
Tremendous value for money: a warm, engaging, gorgeous, tarry, sweaty wine of ripe figs and blackcurrant with a subtle liquorice finish. A chewy delight.

Rosemount Cabernet Sauvignon 1989	13	£D

Shiraz n.v. (Safeway)   15   £B
Fantastic value for a mite over £3. Nice, big, minty, fruity, gingery, red wine. Spicy, muscular yet light. An Oz bobby-dazzler. This is one of those modern wines which travels in bulk from Australia to France to be bottled and bagged-in-box and then hops across the Channel to Safeway's shelves. This rough passage has a great effect on this very contemporary wine, improving it and, paradoxically, recalling the age-old habit of sending wine on a sea voyage to mature.

Taltarni Cabernet Sauvignon 1985   12   £E
Extraordinary full, rich wine which needs time to develop
its genius. The '83 was fully developed and superb but is
now sold out. The '85 has its tannins sorting themselves
out to become eventually smooth and deliciously oily. The
wine has a great future.

Taltarni Shiraz 1988   13   £D
This might well develop some charming manners, given
time to reflect on Safeway's shelves.

The Magill Estate 1987   13   £F
Big wine, big price. Only for serious wine buffs with fat
heads and fat wallets.

**Wolf Blass Yellow Label Cabernet Sauvignon
1988**   13   £D

AUSTRALIAN WINE – *white*

Cru Australis Sauvignon Blanc 1991   12   £B

Eileen Hardy Selection Chardonnay 1988   10   £F

Hardy Collection Chardonnay 1990   13   £D
Rhubarb, peaches and bananas. Very good with rich fish
dishes and tuna salads.

Hardy's Gewürztraminer/Riesling 1991   15   £C
What a wonderful, crazy, turn-the-world-on-its-head
bottle of wine! A fabulous aperitif, a terrific partner for
hard fruit, and maybe even an interesting companion for
heavily smoked ham and spinach salad. But best of all, this
hugely spicy, fruity, cuttingly lemonic patchwork quilt of a

wine is superb with just a book for company. But it has to be a book as out of the ordinary, as modern and as grippingly brilliant, with a touch of acerbic bitterness, as the wine. My vote goes to Helen Zahavi's *Dirty Weekend.*

Jacob's Creek Semillon/Chardonnay 1989   12   £C

Jamiesons Run Chardonnay 1990 (half)   13   £C
Looks like an Anita Brookner book-jacket, sounds like a Jeffrey Archer novel – but this wine is easier to swallow than either. It costs, though.

Mitchelton Marsanne Reserve 1989   13   £D

Moondah Brook Chenin Blanc 1989   12   £C

Orlando RF Chardonnay 1988 and 1989   12   £C

Plantagenet Muscat Bindoon 1990   13   £D
Great sweet, citric aperitif or dessert wine with fresh apples or pears.

**Rosemount Chardonnay 1990,
Oak-Matured**   13   £D

Rosemount Roxburgh Chardonnay 1988   14   £G
Cor blimey, this is like a flash white burgundy with a mite more tasty and concentrated fruit to it. But who can afford to drink it?

Rosemount Show Reserve 1990   14   £E
Splendiferous fruit-laden wine for those equally laden with dosh. A gorgeous mouthful of rich quality fruit.

Semillon n.v. (Safeway)   14   £B
Charming, fruity dry wine with lots of personality.

Semillon/Chardonnay 1990 (Safeway)   14   £C
Full and rounded, ripe and plummy, yet dry. Excellent as
an aperitif or with fish dishes.

The Hardy Collection Chardonnay 1990   12   £D

**Wolf Blass Oak-Matured Chardonnay 1989,
Bilyara Vineyards**   11   £D

AUSTRIAN WINE – *white*

Lenz Moser Pinot Blanc 1991   15   £C
Good dry fruit. Lovely toasted nose, elegant, almost regal.
Excellent structure. That may sound like the sort of
codswallop wine writers jot down as tasting notes, but it's
all true. Translation: this wine is lovely and hugely lap-
uppable. It's also terrific value.

BULGARIAN WINE – *red*

**Cabernet/Merlot Bulgarian Country Wine n.v.
(Safeway)**   13   £A

**Domaine Boyer Cabernet Sauvignon n.v.
(3-litre box)**   14   £F
Rich, woody, raisiny yet dry. A smashing box of vinous
tricks offering a great glass of wine for approx. 43p.

BULGARIAN WINE – *white*

Bulgarian Country Wine n.v. (Safeway)   12   £A

CHILEAN WINE – *red*

Don Maximiano Cabernet Sauvignon 1988   12   £D
You can spot Don Maximiano by his very odd nose.

CHILEAN WINE – *white*

Caliterra Sauvignon Blanc 1991   15   £B
Simply one of the classiest, most satisfying sauvignon blancs for the money on earth. And not without its own intriguing individuality, for the wine-makers in Chile's Maipo Valley seem to conjure a new fruit from this grape – a *grapefruit* no less – and it is quite superb. The balance is perfect.

CHINESE WINE – *white*

Tsingtao Riesling 1988   11   £C
Anyone who could spot in a blind tasting that this was made from riesling grapes has to be a genius. I guessed it must be a chardonnay from St Lucia – so much for my expert taste-buds.

ENGLISH WINE – *white*

Tenterden Special Reserve 1989   10   £D

FRENCH WINE – *red*

Abbaye de Tholomies 1989   15   £B
Terrific value for such dry, well-muscled fruit. Supple,
athletic, delicious.

Beaujolais n.v. (Safeway)   11   £C

Beaujolais Villages 1989 (Safeway)   12   £C

Bergerac 1990 (Safeway)   13   £B
Dry, stylish plonk which is excellent value.

Bourgogne Rouge, Oak-Aged 1990
(Safeway)   10   £D
Oak-aged! Oak-aged! What about some mature fruit for
heaven's sake? (Especially at over a fiver a bottle.)

Cabernet Sauvignon 1990, Oak-Aged Vin de Pays
d'Oc (Safeway)   13   £C
Good value for the impressiveness of the style.

Cabernet Sauvignon, Vin de Pays des Coteaux de
l'Ardèche n.v. (Safeway)   13   £B

Cairanne 1990, Côtes du Rhône Villages   13   £C
Good value for a good C-d-R.

Carraudes de Lafite 1987   12   £F

Château Brondelle, Graves 1988   12 £C

Château Canteloup 1989   12 £C

Château Castera 1990   12 £C
This château can produce some of the best-value bordeaux
on the market. But it does need a little time to develop the
woody fruitiness that is its hallmark.

Château Cos Labory 1987   11 £E

Château de Caraguilhes 1989, Corbières   15 £C
The new breed of corbières-makers are setting a fine
example with their reds. This organic representative is one
of the best – a deep red, with surprising complexity to its
aroma and distinct strata to its fruitiness. One of those
organic wines you feel you can actually sense was grown in
rich, dark earth.

Château de la Rivière, Fronsac 1986 (half)   13 £C

Château Duluc, St-Julien 1989   13 £E

Château Haut-Bages Averous, Pauillac 1985   12 £G

Château Jalette 1990   11 £B

Château Joanny, Côtes du Rhône 1990   14 £B
Lovely mouthful of raspberry and chocolate. Brilliant
value.

Château Julien 1989, Minervois (Safeway)   13 £B
Dark, intense colour – biscuity fruit. The wine embraces
the teeth in a very pleasant tannic and vegetal grip which is
nothing if not friendly.

Château Kirwan, Margaux 1987   12 £E

Château La Lagune, Haut-Médoc 1987   13   £F
Needs time to develop the fullness and gracious richness
this Médoc classically displays but, even so, you can drink
it now. It will only poison your wallet.

**Château La Salle Poujeaux, Haut-Médoc
1985**   11   £E

Château La Tour de Mons, Margaux 1988   11   £E

Château Laroche Viella 1988   14   £D
A Madiran asking £7 must be something special, and this
wine is. Really, it is like a mature St-Estèphe in style and
feel and, as such, excellent value. It is more approachable
than its Bordeaux cousin, of course, the fruit is softer, but
the aroma is there and so is a decent finish.

**Château Ludon Pomies Agassac,
Haut-Médoc**   10   £D

Château Mendoce, Côtes de Bourg 1989   10   £C

Château Plantey, Pauillac 1988   11   £E

Château Tour de Beaupoil 1990   12   £C

**Châteauneuf-du-Pape, La Source Aux Nymphes
1988**   13   £D
You've got to admit it's a saucy title.

Claret, Oak-Aged 1989 (Safeway)   11   £C

Corbières n.v. (Safeway)   11   £B

Côtes du Rhône n.v. (Safeway)   12   £B

Côtes du Roussillon Villages 1988 (Safeway) 12   £B
Not much in the way of smell, but agreeable plonky fruit.

Côtes du Ventoux n.v. (Safeway) 11 £B

**Domaine Anthéa, Merlot, Vin de Pays d'Oc
1990** 14 £B
Previous vintages of this organic wine were marvellous and
eyebrow-raising value for money, and the 1990 continues
the tradition with a lovely touch of dryness to the fruit and
quiet, understated acidity. Excellent dinner party wine.

**Domaine de l'Amérique, Costières de Nîmes
1990** 15 £B
A whopper of a blackcurrant feast and fantastic value for
money.

Domaine Grange du Pin 1990 13 £B
This syrah from the Languedoc is excellent value.

**Domaine la Tuque Bel-Air, Côtes de Castillon
1988** 13 £C

**Domaine Richeaume, Cabernet Sauvignon
1989** 17 £E
The strongest argument yet constructed for the advantages
of organic wine. This absolute stunner, from Provence, is
not frighteningly expensive for its exquisite tannin and soft
fruit balance. The wine coats the teeth lovingly with dry
fruit and then delivers a lengthy finish of rich sweet blackcurrant. I could drink it till the cows come home; not
owning any cows this suggests I have a lot of drinking to
do.

French Organic Vin de Table n.v. (Safeway) 11 £B

Gévrey Chambertin, Laboure-Roi 1988 10 £F

Hautes Côtes de Beaune 1988 (Safeway) 11 £D

La Petite Eglise, Pomerol 1988   10   £E

Médoc n.v. (Safeway)   11   £C

Minervois n.v. (Safeway)   12   £A

Pauillac, Club des Sommeliers 1988   10   £E

St-Emilion n.v. (Safeway)   12   £C

St-Emilion, Club des Sommeliers 1988   12   £D

**Syrah, Vin de Pays des Coteaux de l'Ardèche n.v.
(Safeway) (3-litre box)**   12   £B

Vin de Pays Catalan n.v. (Safeway)   11   £A

Vin de Pays de l'Ardèche 1990 (Safeway)   13   £A
Good value for money.

**Vin de Pays de la Cité de Carcassonne n.v.
(Safeway)**   13   £A

Vin de Pays de Vaucluse 1990   13   £A
A great food-wine bargain – superb with bangers and mash.
Dry, nicely fruity, with no rough edges, this is a terrific little
wine for the money.

Vin de Pays d'Oc, Oak-Aged 1991   12   £C

FRENCH WINE – *white*

Bergerac Sauvignon 1991 (Safeway)   13   £B
Good value.

Bordeaux Blanc, Oak-Aged 1990 (Safeway)   14   £C
A cheap alternative to white burgundy (oddly but gratifyingly).

Bourgogne Blanc 1990 (Safeway) 10 £D

Cabernet d'Anjou, Rosé n.v. 11 £B

**Chardonnay Vin de Pays des Coteaux de l'Ardèche
1991 (Safeway)** 14 £C
Aged in oak, so they say (equivalent to a motor manufacturer
putting GT on the backside of his car), but they bunged in
some green peppers too, I fancy. Well, anything for a varied
life, and this is certainly an individual plonk and jolly
drinkable too.

**Château Bastor Lamontagne 1989, Sauternes
(half)** 14 £C
Marvellous half-bottle. Jammy, rich and curranty and
enough honey to send Pooh Bear aloft.

Château Canet 1991 13 £C
Organic but not yet orgasmic. A great improvement on the
'90 vintage, and edging towards the delicious.

**Château de la Botinière, Muscadet Sur Lie
1990** 13 £C

Château l'Oiseau, Entre-Deux-Mers 1991 12 £B

Corbières Blanc de Blancs 1990 (Safeway) 12 £B

Côtes du Luberon 1990 (Safeway) 13 £B
Good dry drinking and good value in bottle, magnum and
3-litre bag-in-box. Best value, if you don't want to drink the
wine over several weeks, is the magnum; it offers the wine at
33p a glass as against the bottle at 46p and the box at 44p.

Domaine de l'Aube des Temps 1989 14 £F
This wine is best tasted with your tongue in your cheek, for
it is sheer chutzpah from start to finish – from the marvel-
lously daft name, The Dawn of Time, to the long tall Sally of

a bottle. Oddly, the wine is big, buttery and oaky, yet as subtle as a grand white burgundy, but for all that it is a mere Vin de Pays d'Oc. Who said the French have no sense of humour?

Domaine de Malardeu 1990   14 £C
A sauvignon blanc from 'have yeast culture – will travel' English wine-maker at large in France Hugh Ryman (son of the ex-stationer now Dordogne *vigneron*). This is a nicely concentrated, gooseberry-and-melon wine, with a clean disappearing act. Excellent value.

Domaine Ste-Marie, Côtes du Rhône 1991   15 £C
A rarity not to everyone's taste. It is made from bour-boulenc grapes unblended with any others. This is unusual. I like the wine enormously. It reminds me, utterly without reserve, of warm summer afternoons sitting under the plane trees in Vaison La Romaine, a market town a few miles from Gigondas where the wine is made, enjoying a glass of the best house white of the numerous local cafés. Whether this experience is essential to the subsequent enjoyment of this wine is debatable. But with mussels or fish soup, this wine's fruit and metallic freshness are brilliant.

Gewürztraminer 1990, Turckheim   14 £D
Never cheap, this Alsatian masterpiece is one of the world's great wines, yet it is not generally admired. It is spicy and dry, yet fruity, herby and beautifully fragrant, and it goes superbly well with Peking duck, pork chops with apple sauce, and pear tart. It's none the wurtz for being versatile.

La Coume de Peyre 1991   14 £B
Fruit-salad smell on the nose, huge fruit flavour in the

mouth, this wine has fruit on the brain, yet a delightful dash
of acid keeps the whole in shape and makes for a typical
Côtes de Gascogne in many respects – few have this quality,
though.

Mâcon Vire 1990	12	£C

Meursault 1988, Labourne-Roi (Safeway)	8	£F

Muscat, Cuvée Jose Sala   16   £B
Luscious, honeyed, nougaty stuff which by only one penny
nudges into the B-price-band. It is, then, startlingly
wonderful value. It also nudges your taste-buds into paradise if you have the right dessert with it – fruit meringue, for
instance.

Pinot Blanc d' Alsace 1990	13	£C

Sancerre Domaine de Petits Perriers 1990	10	£E

Sauvignon 1991, Cuvée Ramond   15   £B
Just over three quid, this is some bargain. Okay, the fruit
isn't complex, nor is there a great deal of it (considering the
grapes were late-picked and more juicily packed with fruit),
but it is an attractively balanced wine, dry, grapey and
lemony, and it is truly excellent with fish. And at that price
. . . in these parlous times? Grab some quick!

Sauvignon de Haut Poitou 1990	12	£C

Vin de Pays de Vaucluse 1990   14   £A
See entry for red partner of this wine, and I take nothing of
what I said away except that you can substitute fish and
chips, or even oysters Rockefeller, for the bangers and
mash.

Viognier 1991   15   £C
Rather like a Châteauneuf-du-Pape blanc, with an elegant,

dry apricot structure of fruitiness and silken acidity. Viognier is one of the world's greatest grapes but also one of the
least grown – until recently it blossomed in only a few
dozen acres of the Rhône. This example, from neighbour-
ing Ardèche, is a wine of great style.

Vouvray Demi Sec n.v.   10   £C

GERMAN WINE – *red*

Dornfelder Trocken 1990   14   £C
This once had the most glorious gothic nightmare of typo-
graphy on its label, but some svelte designer's been at it so
that now you can not only read it but you might actually
think of buying it. If this notion catches on, the wine will
soon sell out, and I think it should be kept a closely
guarded secret for *Superplonk* readers' eyes and lips alone,
for it is a smashing glug and excellent value with its cherry,
plum, bilberry and blackcurrant aromas and flavours. A
great big soupy savoury fruit salad. And it's German!

GERMAN WINE – *white*

Auslese 1988 (Safeway)   13   £C
Excellent aperitif to start the evening off.

Bereich Bernkastel, Mosel-Saar-Ruwer n.v.
(Safeway)   12   £B

**Dienheimer Tafelstein Scheurebe Kabinett
n.v.**   13   £C
Doktor Becker's interesting organic wine.

**Gewürztraminer Rheinpfalz Halbtrocken n.v.
(Safeway)**   10   £C

Hock, Deutscher Tafelwein n.v. (Safeway)   10   £A

**Ihringer Winklerberg Gewürztraminer Spätlese
1989**   11   £D

Kabinett 1990 (Safeway)   12   £B

**Leiwener Klostergarten Riesling Spätlese
1988**   15   £C
Text-book riesling. Utterly delicious food-wine (with
smoked fish, say, or Singapore-style noodles with squid)
and it demonstrates at a sip why the riesling is one of the
world's great grape varieties. Lemons, a slight touch of
gunflint, rather quiet fruit, but elegant and mouth-
puckeringly delightful. Excellent value under a fiver.

Morio-Muskat 1990, St Ursula   12   £B

Munsterer Rheinberg Riesling 1991   14   £B
What a price for such a smashing little wine! Lovely lemon
acidity and keen fruit, and it's so youthful, too. Might be
out of this world if put away to mature for some years. But
interesting now with ham dishes and especially with pork
chops and apple sauce.

Rulander Kabinett 1989   14   £C
Dry, light, offering citric herbs on the nose and tongue and
a lovely touch of fruit.

**Ruppertsberger Nussbein Riesling Kabinett
1988**   13   £B
Nice little lemon puff of an aperitif.

Spätlese 1990 (Safeway)   12   £B

St Ursula Pinot Blanc 1990   11   £D

Sylvaner Trocken 1991   14   £B
Lovely woody, herby aroma, and good fruit. Excellent
value for money.

GREEK WINE – *red*

Xinomavro Naoussis 1989   15   £C
The first word is the grape variety, the second the area in
Macedonia where it is grown. Luckily, Safeway saves us
ignorant monoglot Brits from having to pronounce either,
since we can grab this wonderful wine off its shelf and stuff
it in our trolley without a word passing our lips. Instead, we
must put it to our lips and experience a warm, woody wine,
herby with blackcurrant and very well-developed fruit,
which is quite sublime with Greek sausages and suchlike.
A real bargain wine for Sunday lunches.

HUNGARIAN WINE – *red*

Merlot, Villany Region n.v. (Safeway)   13   £A
Usual excellent merlot – soft, fruity, attractive and very
good value for money.

Villany 1991   15 £B
Soft as a harem cushion and plump with lashings of voluptuous fruit. Quite fantastic value for money.

HUNGARIAN WINE – *white*

Dry Muscat, Nagyrede n.v.   14 £B
Bit of a sharp finish cuts across the terrific muscat smell
and taste, and sure-footed dryness, but for all that, great
value for money. A first-rate aperitif.

Gyongyos Chardonnay 1991   14 £B
Outstanding value. Finely fruity, rich and full, and it
finishes strongly. Another winner from wine-maker Hugh
Ryman, the greatest English discoverer since David Liv-
ingstone.

Gyongyos Estate Sauvignon Blanc 1991   15 £B
This glorious combo of old world acidity and new world
fruit is the result of Hugh Ryman's sure-fingered touch
and he even throws in a dandy little lemon finish for good
measure. Oh yes, a terrific wine. Oh yes, a terrific price. I
only question where this style of wine-making, in spite of
its practitioner's avowed desire to make wine which is true
to the individual fruit character of its grape varieties, will
eventually lead; for whether it is practised in France,
China, Australia, America, and now Hungary, will it not
iron out regional differences and quirks? Will it not leave
us with one international taste which, however worthy and
however much truly superb value, is as characterless, as
'invented' as esperanto? Only asking.

ISRAELI WINE – *red*

**Carmel Cabernet Sauvignon Samson Region n.v.
(Kosher)**   12 £C
An interesting curiosity; dry and respectably clothed in
fruit.

ISRAELI WINE – *white*

Carmel Dry Muscat 1991   10 £B
Eyeless in Gaza indeed. And also hairless. But then the wine
comes, so it says, from the 'Samson region'. It smells
heavenly, and is perhaps a wine best recommended for tee-
totallers – they can keep their noses in the glass but not
venture further.

Yarden Chardonnay 1990   14 £D
Good Lord! So this is what the chosen people get up to on
the Golan Heights: choosing to make a chardonnay of no
mean quality and style.

ITALIAN WINE – *red*

Bardolino n.v. (Safeway)   13 £B

Camigliano 1986, Montalcino   13 £E
You like drinking old chocolates at a tenner a box? This is
your tipple and delicious you will find it.

Chianti n.v. (Safeway) 12 £B

Chianti Classico 1990, Rocca delle Macie 13 £C

Nebbiolo del Piemonte 1986 (Safeway) 12 £D
An enthralling curiosity, this barrel-aged northerner. It's as brown as old boots but very sweet-natured, and fruity to the point of Christmas-pudding-curranty richness. Great with smelly cheese and might be interesting with game. But very expensive.

Salice Salentino Riserva 1986 15 £C
This wine comes from Puglia in the heel of Italy (though *salice* means willow, so make of that what you will) but it is very far from down-trodden. Rich, tarry, nicely mature, it dallies between soupy fruit and a thrusting acid balance which together make for great style and great taste. One of the handsomest Italians in the store.

Sangiovese di Romagna n.v. 14 £B
The price is promising, the bottle looks intriguing, the smell's like old carpet slippers but the taste! Oh, the taste! Apples and plums, not sweet but rich and rounded, converge to an elegant finish. Delicious wine.

Sicilian n.v. (Safeway) 15 £B
Great rubbery fruit and soothing acidity. Terrific little plonk and a terrific little price. If Bacchus forced us mortals to choose one wine we had to drink with pasta (especially with tomato and basil sauce, or burnt bacon bits) this one would be it.

Tenuta San Vito 1990, Chianti 14 £C
Drier and more austere than is conventional with the type, but then it says it's an organic wine so that must be the reason. Rather expensive for the type, too, but presumably

the same reason can be cited. But an excellent chianti for all that.

Teroldego Rotagliano 1990   13   £C
From Trentino in Northern Italy, this wine, like the terol-dego grapes which make it, is peculiar to the area. Has some pleasant chewy fruit, but I suspect it's asleep and will wake up with a roar in a year or so.

Valpolicella n.v. (Safeway)   12   £B

Valpolicella Classico 1988 'Vigneti Marano'   14   £C
Lovely light wine. Striking balance of acid and fruit makes it good to chill, like a beaujolais, to enjoy with salads and charcuterie.

ITALIAN WINE – *white*

Chardonnay 1990, Grumello del Monte   14   £E
The man from del Monte he say *si!* But don't forget your wallet – although this fine, distinguished wine does have the balance of subtle melony fruit and lemony acidity to justify asking a lot for the privilege of drinking it.

Chardonnay del Triveneto 1990 (Safeway)   13   £C

Fontana Candida Frascati Superiore Secco 1991   11   £C

Orvieto Classico Secco 1990 (Safeway)   12   £B

Pinot Grigio del Triveneto 1990 (Safeway)   13   £B

Sicilian Dry n.v.   11   £B

Soave n.v. (Safeway)   10   £B

Soave Classico, Monteleone 1990   14   £C
Lemons, nuts and melons. What more could you ask of a
real classico soave?

Verdicchio delle Marche 1991 (Safeway)   12   £B

LEBANESE WINE – *red*

Château Musar 1985   12   £D
Seven quid a bottle now, near as dammit. Oh, for the days
of Musar under a fiver and vintages one felt over the moon
about. Maybe this vintage needs more time but it'll have to
go some to catch the '83, which was sublime.

NEW ZEALAND WINE – *white*

Millton Vineyard Chardonnay 1990   14   £E
This organic wine has improved in bottle over the past year
to reveal some signs of gorgeous characterization and
layers of complex flavouring.

Millton Vineyard Sauvignon 1991   12   £E
Well, it is organic.

Montana Sauvignon Blanc 1990,
Marlborough   11   £C

Tauru Valley Müller-Thurgau 1991   12   £C

Wairu River Sauvignon Blanc 1991   12   £D
Reminds me of my mother's cologne to smell and my
father's shaving-soap to taste (plus more than a dash of
lime). Some wine writers think this is the bee's knees. I
think it's pricey but it is excellent with shellfish and the
like.

PORTUGUESE WINE – *red*

Bairrada 1987 (Safeway)   15   £C
Five years old, my life. Such great ripe fruit, such teeth-
clinging dryness, such cutting acidity. For the money, quite
a wine: like figs and tar and lime pastilles.

PORTUGUESE WINE – *white*

Bairrada Reserva 1990   13   £D

ROMANIAN WINE – *red*

Prahova Cabernet Sauvignon 1988   15   £B
This is absurd. The wine's four years old for God's sake,
and it costs about the same as a four-hour-old packet of
fags. They must be desperate for foreign currency in
Romania. You could decant this brilliant, smelly, dry,
classy great treat of a wine into crystal glassware, and most

of us would happily glug away thinking we were putting down some fancy produce from one of those French châteaux with a headless eighteenth-century aristocrat haunting the west wing.

ROMANIAN WINE – *white*

Tamaioasa Pietroasele 1986 13 £C
An interesting touch of stale cabbage (or is it sandals worn by the grape pressers?) with the fruit. Worthy, elegant wine for creamy, fruity puds.

SOUTH AFRICAN WINE – *red*

De Helderberg Cabernet Sauvignon 1991 13 £C

Kanonkop Pinotage 1989 13 £E

SOUTH AFRICAN WINE – *white*

Sauvignon Blanc, Vredendal 1991 12 £B

SPANISH WINE – *red*

Cariñena 1987 (Safeway) 13 £B

Don Darias n.v.   14   £B
Great bargain. Lovely, warm, woody (but more balsa than
heavy oak), fruity, with a totally charming personality.

Navajas Rioja 1985   14   £C
A year on oak, yes, but not vanilla-sodden as a result –
light and deliciously fruity.

Raimat Merlot 1988   12   £D
I love Raimat wines, but for the life of me I cannot
understand why I fail to rate this merlot higher.

Raimat Tempranillo 1988   15   £D
On the nose it is toasty, oaky, blackcurrant and delish.
On the palate there are elegant tannins and lush, controlled berried fruits. The finish is figgy. A marvellous, ripe
wine for spicy Spanish chorizo-dominated food.

Rioja Crianza 1988 (Safeway)   12   £C

Valdepenas 1986   14   £B
Gracious me, yet another wine trumpeting its oak-ageing.
The phrase is becoming as commonplace as 'no artificial
ingredients', which, as a guide to quality, a wine label
could just as meaningfully employ. Not that this wine is
poor. On the contrary, it is like a light rioja in style, with
its pleasant touch of vanilla from all that oak, and it is
fruity, dry and extremely good value for such maturity.

Valencia 1990 (Safeway)   10   £B

SPANISH WINE – *white*

Don Darias n.v.   14   £C
Dry, clean, fruity and very appealing as a thirst-quaffer or as
a fish wine.

La Mancha 1991 (Safeway)   14   £B
Quixotic by label, quixotic in spirit; for with its happy, herby
aroma, hammy fruit and firm finish it tilts at the windmills of
pricier wines and compares very well.

Penedes 1991 (Safeway)   12   £B

Rioja Rosé 1991 (Safeway)   13   £B

Vino de Valencia Dry n.v. (Safeway)   14   £A
Outstanding value for money for a clean, dry, fruity wine
with the temerity to be almost elegant. Deservedly one point
more than last year, for the wine gets better and better.

USA WINE – *red*

**Christian Brothers Napa Valley Cabernet Sauvignon
1986**   13   £D

**Quady Elysium Black Muscat 1989, California
(half)**   10   £D
This exaggerated style shows cinnamon and cloves and
blackberry jam. A curiosity to drink with God knows what.

Ridge Paso Robles Zinfandel 1989   16   £E
Irresistibly tooth-seducing, lip-smackin' liquid, even though
it smells as high, wide and handsome as the inside of Gary

Lineker's fruity left boot after a European Cup match.
Great fat clodfuls of earthy plums, cherries and goodness
knows what else pulse through this wine, and it has gusty
acidity to smooth the whole thing out so it affords a mellow
satisfaction like cello music. I know it's expensive, and I
appreciate the zinfandel is a rogue American grape from
who knows where, but, believe me, I'd choose this wine
over many more famous ones.

USA WINE – *white*

Californian White n.v. (Safeway)   14   £A
Not as popular as it deserves it be (or as understood; at one
wine-tasting I went to I overheard several so-called experts
pompously exclaiming their dislike of this wine). It is certainly built to travel well, for it comes from California yet is
bottled in France. This heretical journey is upsetting to
those romantics who believe that all wine should be bottled
within 6 feet of the vineyard exit. This wine seems
unbruised by its mileage: bright with fruit yet clean-
finishing, it is typical of many excellent, well-made Safeway wines which offer outstanding value for money.

YUGOSLAVIAN WINE – *red*

Milion Pinot Noir 1989, Vranje   14   £A
A delicious, light pinot noir with a vegetal biscuity fruitiness. Fantastic value for money.

YUGOSLAVIAN WINE – *white*

Laski Rizling (Safeway) (1 litre)	10	£C

SPARKLING WINE/CHAMPAGNE

Albert Etienne n.v. (Safeway) — 13 £F

Albert Etienne Brut 1985 (Safeway) — 12 £G

Albert Etienne Rosé n.v. (Safeway) — 12 £G

Angas Brut Rosé n.v. — 15 £D
Fabulous value for anyone planning celebrations at which
rosé champagne is *de rigueur* – the money saved can be
spent on a marriage guidance counsellor for the happy
couple or, if the event be a wake, the dead will probably
come back for it specially, just to get their hands on such
pretty, delicious wine with such determined bubbles.

Blancs de Blancs Brut, France n.v. — 13 £C
Excellent value.

Bollinger Special Cuvée Brut n.v. — 12 £H
Over twenty quid – is it worth it? I wish I could respond
with a wholehearted yes, notwithstanding Bollinger's very
particular dry charms.

Cava n.v. (Safeway) (magnum) — 13 £F
Buy it for the style and the big fat magnum.

Chardonnay Spumante n.v. (Safeway) — 13 £D
Very pleasant champagne substitute.

Chartogne-Taillet Champagne Brut n.v.   13   £F

Codorniu Blanc de Blancs 1987 Cava   14   £E
Superbly elegant fizzer. A real find. Has to be bought
instead of champagne. A bargain at this price.

Crémant de Bourgogne Blanc de Blancs n.v.
(Safeway)   13   £D

Cuvée Napa, USA n.v.   14   £E
Compared to a classic brut champagne, which Cuvée Napa
completely resembles in style and feel, this Californian
sparkler is tremendous value for money. This is no surprise, for it is made under the supervision of the Mumm
champagne house of Rheims in a joint venture with the
giant liquor company Seagrams (owners of Oddbins).

Great Western Brut Reserve 1988 and 1989   15   £D
A bargain champagne in all but name (and what does that
count for nowadays?).

Lindauer Brut, New Zealand n.v.   12   £D

Lionel Derens Champagne n.v.   15   £E
A dry but fruity champagne, without the intimidating
acidity of the classic brut examples, this is a very satisfying
tipple and a good price at £8.50.

Sparkling Blackcurrant n.v.   15   £B
This is pure, unadulterated blackcurrant in smell and
taste. This is not surprising since no grape gets a look in,
just blackcurrants. It is great fun and a hilarious addition to
a party or a Christmas lunch – even at 5.55 alcohol.

Vouvray Tête de Cuvée Brut n.v.   12   £D

Sainsbury's

ARGENTINIAN WINE – *red*

Trapiche Cabernet Sauvignon 1986   13   £C

AUSTRALIAN WINE – *red*

**Hunter Valley Cabernet Sauvignon Bin 937
1989**   16   £C
This is some handsome brute. Woody, herby, dry yet
highly charged with lovely berried fruit. The sort of utterly
charming Aussie bastard for whom a lady would leave
home, husband and cellar of slow-maturing claret.

Hunter Valley Shiraz Bin 827 1989   15   £C
Ripe figs and ripe black cherries predominate in this
superb international collaboration between Swiss fermentation equipment, American oak casks and then French oak
casks. The result is a very friendly bottle. It puts its arm
around you and squeezes your taste-buds to death. Yet
though sweet in soul it is dry in character. A lovely long
slurp of sheer delectable fruit.

Orlando St Hugo Cabernet Sauvignon 1987   15   £E
Brash with oaky, deep, rich fruit – a wine with as pene-
tratingly satiny a voice as Paul Robeson singing 'Old Man
River'. Quite marvellous with roast meats with complex
sauces. It was one of several wines used to test candidates

in the Sainsbury's/BBC *Good Food Magazine* Wine Taster
of the Year competition, which I helped judge, and most of
the hopefuls thought it was a venerable old claret. A con-
clusion, I must say, I might well have reached myself had I,
like they, been tasting it blind. Watch the solidified tannin
shreds as you open the bottle – they gather like toffeed
sawdust on the end of the cork and the inside neck needs
careful cleaning before you pour the wine. This horrifies
the sanitized Americans, but it's good news for those of us
who dislike our wine overfiltered.

RF Cabernet Sauvignon Orlando 1989	12	£C

Shiraz/Cabernet n.v. (Sainsbury's)	12	£B

Good price for an interesting wine showing both greenness
and ripeness. A wine of unsettled demeanour.

South-East Australian Shiraz/Cabernet n.v.	15	£B

Fabulous big wine with masses of tarry fruit, but not the
aggressive or ugly sort. This is very classy tar. (The sort on
Buck House roof.)

AUSTRALIAN WINE – *white*

Chardonnay 1991 (Sainsbury's)	13	£C

Chardonnay Cranswick Estate 1991	12	£C

Good old-fashioned stuff. Rich, oaky, pineappley. Has to
be drunk, like a sauce, with food – though whether the
right type of food has yet been invented is open to
question.

Chenin Semillon n.v. (Sainsbury's)	12	£B

Hunter Valley Chardonnay 1991, Denman Estate   14   £C

This was one of the answers in this year's Sainsbury's/BBC *Good Food Magazine* Wine Taster of the Year competition, well won by a gynaecologist from Shrewsbury who gave delivery of a near-immaculate paper (I was a judge, so I know this). The question had to do with country of origin and grape variety and I think the answer is difficult with this wine because it is not yer typical Aussie fruit gangbang. It is quite superior stuff with a great touch of wood, and excellent fruit and acid balance. A touch snooty, in fact.

Jacob's Creek Semillon/Chardonnay 1990   12   £C

Mitchelton Botrytis Affected Rhine Riesling 1983   10   £C

Not enough power for a dessert wine but has some aperitif promise.

Mitchelton Marsanne 1988   12   £D

Semillon Riverina n.v.   13   £B

A bargain taste-bud opener and conversation starter – you can tell your spellbound guests how the grape juice is inoculated with *Saccharomyces bayanus* yeast, which kick-starts the fermentation.

South-East Australian Chenin/Chardonnay n.v.   14   £C

Like leather patches on a woolly jumper. Normally, I loathe the design, but this one works extremely well, with the chenin's wet-wool taste blending nicely with the new leather of the chardonnay. Plummy, melony, lemony, with a touch of mango on the finish. Those hairy-chested Australians no doubt drink it instead of fruit juice for breakfast.

South-East Australian Chenin/Semillon n.v. 16 £B
Absolutely adorable blend of dry woody fruit, citrus, lychee
and plums. Fabulous concoction, rich, deep and very satisfying. Would be great with fresh oysters or moules mar-
inière (especially if the chef has bunged in lots of garlic and
lemon-grass).

AUSTRIAN WINE – *white*

Bouvier Trockenbeerenauslese 1989 (half)   13 £D
Not as pungent as its German counterpart. It ought to be
aged more to develop its undoubted complex character.
Still, if you're feeling extravagant, and someone's given you
a pound of strawberries, treat yourself.

Winzerhaus Grüner Veltliner 1991   15 £B
I like to think my grandpa, Ignatz, as he barbered late-
nineteenth-century Viennese nobility, drank this wine, but
this is a romantic notion which you must believe has played
no part in my liking of the stuff. Lovely broad, supple fruit,
keen acid, it is a revelation and a great rebuttal to those
bores who say the only decent things to come out of Vienna
are Mozart and wiener schnitzel.

BULGARIAN WINE – *red*

Bulgarian Cabernet Sauvignon n.v.
(Sainsbury's)   13 £B

Bulgarian Country Red n.v.   15   £B

Here I go again, having to swallow my words. I tasted last
year's batch of this wine, made from cabernet sauvignon
and cinsault grape varieties, early in the year and never
rated it highly enough to include it in the book. Nine
months later BBC Radio 'Food and Drink' programme
put me on the spot when they asked me to taste it again and
the wine had changed out of all recognition. It was simply
glorious. The new batch of the wine I'm tasting in June
gives me the feeling that when this book comes out in
November the same gremlins will be at work pushing the
wine to even greater heights. Here's hoping.

Stambolovo Merlot Special Reserve 1986   12   £D

BULGARIAN WINE – *white*

Bulgarian Country White n.v.   12   £A

Ignore the just-opened-door-of-the-spin-drier aroma and
go for the freshly laundered and well-scrubbed fruit – this
is the wine's most forward feature.

**Welsch-Riesling n.v. (Sainsbury's) (3-litre
box)**   14   £E

No, the subjects of Big Ears' principality are not in cahoots
with the East Europeans. Welsch-Riesling is a grape,
grown near the banks of the Danube, and it makes a clean
yet rounded wine, rather in the chardonnay mould but
without the layers of flavour. Still, the box is great value for
parties or to keep in the fridge for when you fancy the odd
glass.

CHILEAN WINE – *red*

Caliterra Cabernet Sauvignon 1988   14   £C
One of Chile's whispering wonders – lovely, quiet, nothing
flashy. A book wine (i.e. can be drunk alone without food).

CHILEAN WINE – *white*

Chilean Sauvignon Blanc n.v.   14   £B
Delicate, clean, perfectly weighted fruit, not sharp. Good
value.

Santa Rita Chardonnay 1990   13   £D
Impressive and a fine mouthful, but at this price suffers
severe competition.

CHINESE WINE – *white*

Tsingtao Chinese Chardonnay 1988   12   £C
An interesting wine which is not as much of a curiosity as it
sounds. It tastes like old-fashioned Australian chardonnay,
but then an Aussie wine-maker put it together.

ENGLISH WINE – *white*

Hastings, Carr Taylor n.v.   14   £C
Stocked only in five branches in Sussex, and the English

wine I like best. It has an Alsatian feel to it, with perhaps not quite that region's barking acidity, but nevertheless a well-balanced, well-made specimen of some style. (See under Waitrose.)

Lamberhurst Sovereign n.v. 12 £C
Stocked only in five branches in Kent.

Three Choirs Seyval Reichensteiner 1990 12 £C
Stocked only in five branches in Gloucestershire.

FRENCH WINE – *red*

Anjou Rouge n.v. (Sainsbury's) 12 £B

Beaujolais n.v. (Sainsbury's) 10 £C

Beaujolais-Villages, Château des Vergers 1990 10 £C

Bergerac Rouge n.v. (Sainsbury's) 12 £B

Bergerie de l'Arbous 1989 15 £C
This is a stunning blend of grenache and syrah grape varieties and the bottle is very easy to overlook among Sainsbury's 'Vintage Selection' of pricier wines as it is not the least bit pricey, looks odd, and comes from the Languedoc, an area which many people still regard as a backwater, failing to wake up to the fact that some of the most interesting new French wines are coming from there. Lovely soft fruit, handsome touch of wood, Bergerie is exceptional and an outstanding bargain.

Cabernet Sauvignon Selection Skalli n.v. 14 £C
Excellent value – elegant, mature, fruity yet dry.

**Cabernet Sauvignon Vin de Pays d'Oc n.v.
(3-litre box)**   12   £F

Cahors, Château Les Bouysses 1987   12   £C
Subdued fruit, chewy wine. Craggy and coarse but a genuine character. Smashing with cheese – the acidity of the
wine tackles it beautifully.

Cahors n.v. (Sainsbury's)   14   £B
Bargain price for a rich, dark wine which would, I suspect,
be great with grilled lamb chops and herbs.

**Château Arnaud, Haut-Médoc 1987
(magnum)**   13   £F
Very dryish fruit. Good partner for all roast meats.

Château Artigues Arnaud 1988, Pauillac   13   £D

Château Barreyres, Haut-Médoc 1988   14   £D
The bitter fruit is well harnessed by the aroma. A very
good-value wine, given its seriousness.

Château Bel Evêque, Corbières 1989   14   £C
Aromatically, this is more intriguing than my adored Voulte
Gasparets (q.v.). Skilfully blended from grenache, syrah,
carignan and mourvèdre, and oak-aged (with this having a
most felicitous effect on the mourvèdre), it has very good
fruit which just fails to explode with flavour as does the other
wine. Nevertheless, an excellent wine for the money.

Château Bellevue la Forêt 1990   13   £B

Château Blaignan, Médoc 1986 (magnum)   14   £F
Distinguished, biscuity, fruity flavour – distinct blackberry
nose. Elegant. Some finesse. Love the big bottle.

Château Bonnet 1988 (magnum)   14   £F
I love big bottles like this for candle-lit suppers when two

of you either want romance on a budget or to get sloshed in style.

Château Cantemerle, Haut-Médoc 1987	12	£G

Château Dauzac, Margaux 1985	13	£F

Château de Camensac 1985 (magnum)   12   £H
I do not think this wine is expensive, nor do I think it is as brilliant as it will be in six or seven years or even ten. It is a fifth growth, as classified in 1855 (which means different things to different people these days), and by the end of the century this particular bottle may well perform like a first.

Château de Gallifet, Cairanne 1989, Côtes du Rhône Villages   13   £C

Château de Pizay Morgon 1988	12	£D

Château de Roques 1989   13   £B
Excellent for dinner parties.

Château La Vieille Cure, Fronsac 1988   15   £D
This is an instantly likeable bordeaux at a bargain price for such classy tippling. Bouquet: blackcurrant on a bed of cedar wood. Taste: crumpled satin. Finish in the throat: softness and richness. The store says the wine 'has a long youthful finish' – a phrase they must have borrowed from one of the calling cards which certain ladies in my area of London are given to papering phone boxes with – this may, or may not, give you a clue to the wine's ready sensuality.

Château la Voulte Gasparets, Corbières 1989 15   £C
One of the great stars of last year's edition of this book was the 1988 vintage of this wine to which I also devoted a whole column in the *Weekend Guardian*. This '89 is coming along, and will improve, but it is still a humdinger of a

fruity specimen, with herbs and a faint touch of spice. Woody, dry, but never coarse, this is a terrific corbières and demonstrates the increasing quality, and outstanding value for money, that this area is providing.

Château Lyonnat 1986 (magnum)   14 £F
This is a Lussac-St-Emilion. This practice of attaching a village name to a more illustrious neighbour is widespread in France and the commercial advantages are obvious. However, this Lussac is so good that it has been of premier cru St-Emilion status in quality, if not in taxonomy, for longer than I can remember. Lyonnat is an excellent classy, supple wine and in its magnum it is doubly appealing. I am no longer able to contemplate opening such a bottle and a book (Hazlitt's essays go with it particularly well), and consuming both, so this is my wine for dinner parties when merely lifting the bottle gives cause for satisfaction.

Château Maucaillou, Moulis 1988   13 £F

Château Rozier, St-Emilion 1989   14 £E
Delicious, calm, smelly and fruity. Oaky and vegetal, yet fruitily dry. Very cosy, soft wine of some distinction. Class act. Mature. Not as friendly as some – demands that attention, and respect, are paid to it. Won't let you get away with a hasty slurp, you have to think about it. (So reads my tasting note.)

Château Tourteau-Chollet, Graves 1986   13 £D
This has elegance and class: dry fruit, not overloaded or tannic. A touch of burnt wood on the finish.

Claret Bordeaux Supérieur n.v. (Sainsbury's)   14 £B
This must be among the best-value wines that claret lovers can get their hands on, since it is nothing more nor less

than a cabernet sauvignon of simple construction yet undeniable pedigree.

Clos du Marquis 1986, St-Julien 14 £F

Ripe melon in this one. Can't figure out how it got there. And goodness, how they charge for it. It's a delicious bordeaux for all that, and a second growth of the legendary Léoville-Lascases. (It's worth pointing out, however, that it is not one of those second growth 'opportunist' wines popular with Bordeaux châteaux' marketing men over the past decade; Marquis has been a Lascases' sub for ninety years.)

Corbières, Château St-Auriol 1988 (Sainsbury's) 13 £C

Côte-Rôtie, Delas 1987 11 £F

Côtes du Rhône Villages, Beaumes de Venise n.v. 14 £C

Since the village of Beaumes has become so closely linked with dessert wine, the fine reds made here do not attract as much attention or such high price-tags. This wine is a case in point. Made by the excellent local wine co-op, it has the usual dry, slightly wet-earth fruit well supported by plum and cherry undertones. An excellent food-wine, it seems to kow-tow to whatever is on the plate – be it a truffle omelette or a hamburger.

Côtes du Roussillon n.v. (Sainsbury's) 13 £B

An excellent-value-for-money, simply constructed, dry country wine.

Crozes-Hermitage n.v. (Sainsbury's) 12 £C

Good value for a goodish, rich, dark, full wine of woody fruit. Has to be drunk with food.

Cuvée la Source, Coteaux d'Aix en Provence
1986   10   £C
This is an oddity, since it is Château Vignelaure in all but
name and Vignelaure was one of the first great, organic
Provence reds. I was possibly the first foreigner to drink
this wine way back in the mid-1970s before it became
famous and exported and deservedly sought-after. This
cuvée is drinkable but it's pricey for the style, which
seems loosely assembled. Maybe the wine will improve
over the next six months. (I tasted it in early '92.)

Domaine Chancel, Syrah 1991   12   £C
Interesting toffee-apple touch to the fruit.

Domaine du Colombier, Chinon 1990   12   £C
Previous vintages of this liquid velvet have been among
the glories of the Sainsbury's wine list.

Domaine du Révérend, Corbières 1989   14   £C
Tar and rose-water entwined with the soft berried fruit
make this the third brilliant corbières on Sainsbury's
shelves.

Fiefs de Lagrange 1987, St-Julien   15   £E
Grassy on the nose, then the richness and complexity
wallop the palate and you think, 'God, this is good old-
style claret without tannic unfriendliness.' A very com-
panionable wine with fine food: elegant, distinguished in a
slightly raffish sense and very warmly fruity.

Fitou, Les Guèches 1989   13   £B
Bright, plummy fruit.

Fleurie, La Madone 1991   12   £D

Hautes Côtes de Beaune, La Dalignière 1989 14 £D
Light, delicious burgundy, with everything as it should be
– except the price.

Juliénas, Château des Capitans 1990 11 £D

Le Petit Cheval, St-Emilion Grand Cru 1988 11 £G
Second wine of the legendary Château Cheval Blanc. A lot
of loot. Not a lot of boot. But drinkable. Disappointing for
the price. A well-made but ineffably dull wine; but laid
down it will improve greatly. Can you afford to wait till the
kids grow up?

Les Forts de Latour, Pauillac 1983 14 £G
Attractive, forward style; gamey and fruity, rather in the
manner of a velvety burgundy. The most distinguished
glassful at the tasting of second wines at which I drank it,
but it is a lot of money. It's the name you're paying for;
Forts de Latour is not Château Latour but another wine,
from a separate stretch of wines, made by the same people
– hence its designation 'second wine'. If you want the
name Latour on your dinner table, however, you'll have to
pay for it.

Marsannay 1987, Chenu 14 £D
A highly drinkable, very good burgundy. Will improve for
some years if cellared. Very good value.

Minervois n.v. (Sainsbury's) 15 £B
This wine gave me a headache. But not from any over-
indulgence in its bargain structure of delicious soft fruit
wrapped in velvet. It was Sainsbury's temporary reduction
in its price to £1.99. As *Guardian* readers flocked to buy
the wine a week before the offer closed, on my recom-
mendation, they found the offer *had* closed. The postman
delivered the angry letters by fork-lift truck. I spent two

weeks replying to every reader, as did Sainsbury's apologizing for their error and making recompense, but how will I ever make up for that lost fortnight? Your Lordship, you owe me one (two, in fact).

Mondot, St-Emilion 1989	13	£E

Moulin à Vent, Cave Kuhnel 1990 11 £D
Only two branches stock this wine.

Nuits St-Georges, Clos de Thorey 1985 12 £G

Pavillon Rouge du Château Margaux 1988 14 £G
Rose-water, blackcurrants and ripe figs – elegance, fullness, distinction.

Red Burgundy, Pinot Noir n.v. (Sainsbury's) 10 £C

Réserve de la Comtesse 1988, Pauillac 10 £F
Sour finish which spoils a fair wine at a huge price.

Savigny-les-Beaune 1987 13 £E
Comforting rather than spectacular.

St-Chinian, Domaine St-Anne 1990 14 £B
This employs the ubiquitous Southern French grape varieties, syrah and carignan, along with the increasingly popular mourvèdre, to great effect. The wine has good, firm fruit, is well balanced, and has the style to go well with posh roast lamb dishes. As such, it may stimulate not merely the gastric juices but also comments of the 'Goodness, under three quid, I can't believe it' kind.

**Vin de Pays de la Cité de Carcassonne,
Domaine Sautes le Bas 1991** 12 £B

Vin de Pays de la Dordogne n.v. 12 £B

FRENCH WINE – *white*

Alsace Gewürztraminer n.v. (Sainsbury's)	13	£C
Alsace Pinot Blanc n.v. (Sainsbury's)	13	£C
Alsace Riesling n.v. (Sainsbury's)	12	£C
Bergerac Blanc n.v. (Sainsbury's)	13	£B
Blush n.v. (Sainsbury's Rosé)	11	£B
Bordeaux Sauvignon n.v. (Sainsbury's)	12	£B

Chablis Premier Cru, Côte de Lechet 1990 14 £E
If you want a classic chablis, this is it. Lean and green, fat and fruity – only chablis pulls off this remarkable double act with such style, in such uniquely satisfying proportions.

Chablis, Brocard 1990 (Sainsbury's)	12	£D
Chablis, Daniel Colbois 1990	11	£D

Chablis, St-Céline 1990 15 £D
Classic stuff.

Chais Baumière Sauvignon Blanc 1991 14 £C
Made by Bill and Pete in Southern France, and very well this Aussie twosome perform, coaxing nicely vegetal, subtly rich sauvignon character from the grapes.

Chardonnay, Skalli n.v. (Sainsbury's) 13 £C
Good, firm, fruity, clean. And good value.

Château de Davenay, Montagny Premier Cru 1990 12 £D

Château Mayne des Carmes, Sauternes 1989 14   £F
Second wine of Château Rieussec, but playing second
fiddle to no one with regard to flavour and complexity.

Corbières Blanc n.v. (Sainsbury's)   12   £B

Coteaux du Languedoc n.v. (Sainsbury's)   14   £B
Another great, nutty, fruity, clean-finishing Sainsbury's
white wine at a bargain price.

Coteaux du Layon, Château du Breuil 1989 14   £D
Delightful light dessert wine for soft fruits and creamy
puds.

Côtes de Duras n.v. (Sainsbury's)   13   £B
Very pleasant appley, wet-wool fruit.

Domaine Belle Croix 1989, Coteaux de St-Bris,
Bourgogne Aligote   14   £C
This is a white burgundy good and true but it's not a
chardonnay, it's an aligote – a much-maligned grape
variety which has always had a friend in me. This wine is a
perfectly balanced specimen, touched by gracefulness on
the high wire of acidity, strengthened by firm, melony
richness on the low bar of fruitiness. Great stuff.

Domaine des Blancs, Côtes du Luberon
Rosé   14   £B
An admirable example of a deservedly despised genre.
Excellent with smoked fish.

Duc Dupeyron 1990   15   £D
Beautifully distinguished combination of glossy fruit and
fine-grained wood. Lovely temperament, it caresses the
tongue. A classy wine which would be great with grilled
giant prawns or lobster. Indeed, if I were to eat my last
meal tomorrow I could happily settle for that dish with this

wine. (And, interestingly, it is a 70 per cent semillon/30 per cent sauvignon blend, popular with antipodeans. For them, this wine is an object-lesson.)

Gros Plant du Pays Nantais 1990   11   £B
Needs fresh shellfish to be at its most drinkable.

Jurançon Sec 1991   13   £B

Le Sec de Rayne Vigneau 1990   13   £D
Lovely, stylish stuff.

**Mâcon Blanc Villages, Domaine Les Chenevières
1990**   13   £C

**Mâcon Chardonnay, Domaine les Ecuyers
1990**   14   £D
Good price for such an elegant white burgundy. (Other white wine-makers in the area, please note.)

Mouton Cadet 1990   12   £C

**Muscadet de Sèvre-et-Maine Sur Lie, Château de la
Dimerie 1990**   11   £C

Muscat de St-Jean de Minervois n.v.   14   £B
A useful half-bottle of silky dessert wine. Especially welcome with tarts and puds without citric sauces.

Picpoul de Pinet n.v.   12   £C

**Pouilly Fuisse, Domaine Henri Carrette
1989**   12   £E

Pouilly Fumé, Les Chantalouettes 1990   11   £D

**Premières Côtes de Bordeaux 1989, Domaine Tour
du Guet (Sainsbury's)**   13   £C

Premières Côtes de Bordeaux n.v.   11   £C

Puligny Montrachet, Roux 1989   10   £G

**Quincy, Domaine de la Maison Blanche
1990**   12   £C
Nose: clean, invigorating. Palate: lively, green grapes and
lemons. Finish: flinty. Quincy but quirky.

Sancerre, Les Beaux Regards 1991   15   £E
Still one of the classiest sancerres on any supermarket
shelf – gooseberry-fresh and clean, and deliciously dry
with a subtle, melony edge.

**Vin de Pays des Côtes de Gascogne,
Domaine Bordes 1991**   13   £B
Nothing tart about this Bordes.

**Vin de Pays des Côtes du Tarn n.v.
(Sainsbury's)**   13   £B

Vin de Pays d'Oc n.v. (Sainsbury's)   13   £B
Good-value, clean wine.

**Vin de Pays d'Oc Chardonnay n.v.
(3-litre box)**   12   £G
58p a glass is no bad price to pay for a wine with such
pleasant fruit.

Vin de Pays d'Oc Sur Lie 1991   13   £B
The 'sur lie' tells us that the wine has merely been allowed
to pick up flavour and depth, and increased character, from
prolonged contact with its lees: this is excellent value for
such pricey processing.

Vin de Pays du Gers n.v. (Sainsbury's)   13   £B

Vin de Pays du Jardin de la France n.v. 14 £B
One of the nattiest bargains on Sainsbury's shelves. Buy it instead of muscadet and drink with all those things you used to drink muscadet with.

White Burgundy Chardonnay n.v.
(Sainsbury's) 13 £C

GERMAN WINE – *white*

Alsheimer Rheinblick Beerenauslese 1986 15 £E
Pricey, but worth it for the ortega grape's particular honeyed style. Marvellous with any kind of pud, but especially rich, cakey ones. Liquid paradise after dinner.

Auslese Bereich Mittelhaardt
1989 and 1990 (Sainsbury's) (half) 16 £A
What a gift from God this wine is: apples, pears, lychees, lemons. And the half-bottle is a wonderful size and price. Treat yourself to a bottle for lunch and eat with it some soft goat's cheese, grapes and Sainsbury's baguette baked with French flour. You'll go back to work inspired. This is a most beautifully rich, fragrant, fruity wine, cut through with the unique acid gorgeousness of the riesling grape. With ham dishes, or with light fish soups, or with a complex creation like coronation chicken, it is stunningly glorious.

Baden Dry n.v. (Sainsbury's) 15 £B
One of the most interesting of the dry badenese on supermarket shelves, by virtue of the fact that some clever

blighter smuggled some gewürztraminer into the grape
blend, and the result, whilst still dry, is subtly spicy and
fruity.

Erdener Treppchen 1990   14   £D
Wonderful citrus undertones. Great aperitif or with salads.

**Kabinett Rheinhessen 1990, Dalsheimer Burg
Rodenstein (Sainsbury's)**   14   £B
A terrific aperitif for under three quid – lovely, refreshing,
acidic style cut with undertones of herbal softness.

Kaseler Herrenberg 1988   12   £D

Morio-Muskat Rheinpfalz n.v. (Sainsbury's) 12   £B

Niersteiner Gutes Domtal n.v. (Sainsbury's) 12   £A

Riesling Nahe n.v. (Sainsbury's)   12   £B

**Spätlese Mosel-Saar-Ruwer, Bernkasteler
Kurfurstlay 1989 (Sainsbury's)**   12   £C

Trocken Rheinhessen n.v. (Sainsbury's)   11   £B
Inoffensive aperitif providing apples and elderberry on the
nose.

GREEK WINE – *white*

Retsina n.v.   13   £B
One of the bargains in the store. Yes, I know retsina is an
anagram of 'nastier', and that it's made from boxing rings
and old cricket bats, but with Greek-style food, especially
starters, a good retsina is terrific. And this is a good one.

HUNGARIAN WINE – *red*

Merlot n.v. (Sainsbury's)   15   £B
Hugely enjoyable, toffeed cherry and burnt orange-zest
fruit, all soft and cuddly, make this wine one of the best
merlots for under £3 it is possible to pour into a glass. Of
course, the addition of the local grape kekfrankos to the
merlot may be the reason, so pure merlot growers are
entitled to cry 'Foul!' But anyone who expresses such
sentiments upon tasting the wine needs a taste-bud
transplant.

HUNGARIAN WINE – *white*

Gyongyos Estate Chardonnay 1991   15   £B
The care that has gone into making this wine by Hugh
Ryman, peripatetic English wine-maker, is obvious from
aroma, taste, and finish in the throat. If he can make
chardonnay this rich and characterful in the Matra Mountain foothills north of Budapest, what would he do on the
famed slopes of the Côte d'Or?

Hungarian Pinot Blanc n.v. (Sainsbury's)   16   £B
Slightly chalky quality to the rich, soft fruit, but great
glugging nevertheless. One of the store's most remarkable
white wine bargains.

ITALIAN WINE – *red*

Castelgreve Chianti Classico Riserva 1986   14   £D
Ripe, mature, dry. Figgy and full of fruit. Very, very stylish.

Castello di San Polo in Rosso 1987   16   £D
Fantastic classy chianti.

Chianti n.v. (Sainsbury's)   15   £B
A smashing, simple, biscuit-dry and earthily fruity chianti
with vigorous undertones. A fabulous bargain and great
with all kinds of pastas, pizzas and cooked cheesy things.

**Chianti Classico, Barone Ricasoli 1988
(Sainsbury's)   16   £C**
The perfect restraint of the label belies the unrestrained,
all-embracing aromatic fruitiness of a terrific wine.

Lago di Caldaro n.v.   15   £C
One of those utterly charming, effortless fruity Northern
Italian miracles which so few people hear of that it's a
crime. Or not, as the case may be. (Those of us who find
wines like this perfect summer substitutes for the beaujolais we can no longer afford, nor, with its over-sugared
alcohol, wish to drink, think it's splendid that Caldaro's
anonymity keeps the price so low.)

Rosso di Montalcino 1990   13   £E

**San Lorenzo Rosso Conero 1988, Umani
Ronchi   13   £C**

Spargolo 1985   13   £F
Very dry, very pretty, and pongs of asparagus. This vintage
produced barely 20,000 bottles, so only two Sainsbury's
branches stock it.

Valpolicella Classico, Negarine 1989 15 £B
I adore this wine. It has taken the place that beaujolais
used to have in my affections – when that wine was both
affordable and not so rotten with sugar that it was too
alcoholic. In many people's minds, valpolicella is to wine
what Enid Blyton is to literature, so this marvellous
example, with its lovely, umbraceous fruity style dry-edged
with digestive biscuit, is a bargain. Please don't confuse
this wine with Sainsbury's other Valpolicella Classico.
Negarine is the word to look for.

**Valpolicella Classico (Sainsbury's)
(magnum)** 11 £C

**Vino Nobile di Montepulciano, Fattoria di Casale
1988** 13 £D

Winemaker's Choice, Rosso n.v. 11 £B

ITALIAN WINE – *white*

Avignonesi il Marzocco 1989 13 £F
Gorgeous, elegant, pricey – like a tart on the Via Veneto.

**Bianco di Custoza, Castelnuovo, Pasqua 1991
(Sainsbury's)** 13 £B

Bianco Toscano n.v. (Sainsbury's) 13 £B
Excellent aperitif: nice fruit, soft lemon finish.

**Casal di Serra, Verdicchio dei
Castelli Jesi n.v.** 13 £C

Casato delle Macie 1990 13 £C

Chardonnay 1989, Zenato	13	£C
Chardonnay Alto Adige 1991 (Sainsbury's)	14	£C
Chardonnay del Piemonte 1990	13	£C

Chardonnay del Piemonte n.v. (Sainsbury's) 14 £C
Beautiful floral freshness and elegance of fruit.

Cortese Alto Monferrato n.v. (Sainsbury's) 13 £B
Excellent with fish and salad starters.

Garganega Sauvignon 1991 (Sainsbury's)	13	£C
Gavi, Bersano 1991	13	£C

Lugana San Benedetto 1990, Zenato 13 £C
Luxurious lemon ice-cream flavour allied to a zesty freshness makes this a delicious specimen.

Pinot Grigio, Grave del Friuli, Collavini 1990 12 £C
Delicious in its own way, but I wonder if the label provides
more of a talking-point than the wine in the bottle? Perilously close to a fiver a bottle for comfort.

Santa Christina Chardonnay 1990, Zenato 13 £D
Only three branches stock this wine; wisely, perhaps, for
though it is good it is also expensive.

Soave Classico Costalunga, Pasqua 1991
(Sainsbury's) 12 £B

Tocai del Veneto n.v. (3-litre box) 11 £F

Trebbiano di Romagna n.v. (Sainsbury's)
(magnum) 13 £C

Verduzzo del Piave n.v. (Sainsbury's) 14 £B
As lovely as it sounds.

Vernaccia di San Gimignano 1990,
San Quirico 13 £C
A terrific wine with shellfish: dry, gentle, fruity and not
overfull of itself.

Winemaker's Choice n.v. 12 £B

LEBANESE WINE – *red*

Château Musar 1983 17 £D
The magical wine of the Lebanon. (See under Asda for
more details.)

NEW ZEALAND WINE – *red*

Chenin/Chardonnay 1991 (Sainsbury's) 12 £C

Cook's Cabernet/Merlot 1988 12 £C

Cook's Hawkes Bay Sauvignon Blanc 1991 13 £C

Nobilo Chardonnay 1991 13 £C

PORTUGUESE WINE – *red*

Arruda n.v. (Sainsbury's) 15 £B
A great toasted bouquet, herbs on the fruit, and a fair old
lingering, woody finish. One of Sainsbury's great bargains.

Bairrada 1987   13   £B

Dão 1987 (Sainsbury's)   13   £B

Herdada de Santa Marta 1989   14   £C
From the Alentejo area which is slowly asserting itself as
one of the prime vineyard sites in Europe. This wine,
typical of its kind, offers great style at a great price. The
distinctive sweetness, in an essentially dry wine, is genuine
and fresh-fruity and makes the wine perfect with all manner of well-flavoured foods from spicy sausages to chilli
con carne.

Quinta da Bacalhoa 1989   13   £C

ROMANIAN WINE – *red*

Romanian Pinot Noir n.v.   15   £B
Bumping into the glamorous daughter of a cabinet minister
in my local Sainsbury's as she was hunting out wine for a
dinner party, I suggested this one and she turned up her
nose (an expression I felt a great deal of educational
funding had gone into perfecting). I was secretly, and
shamefully, pleased at her 'I couldn't possibly put a bottle
like that on my table', for it meant the wine will never
become fashionable and will therefore stay affordable for
boozers like me who appreciate the absurdity of forking out
under three quid for a pinot noir which has spent between
three and four years in barrel and emerged rich, aromatic
and quite stunningly concentrated. A wine I would
unhesitatingly put among my top ten bargains available
anywhere.

SOUTH AFRICAN WINE – *white*

Chenin Blanc n.v. (Sainsbury's) 14 £B
This is a toothsome bargain – easily the fruitiest non-
French chenin blanc my hoary old taste-buds have ever
had the pleasure of drowning in. I think Nadine Gordimer
is the best companion for it.

Swartland Colombard 1991 11 £B

Vredendal Sauvignon Blanc 1992 12 £B

SPANISH WINE – *red*

La Mancha, Castillo de Alhambra 1991 14 £B
A lovely, stylish fruity/dry wine. Elegantly made. Terrific
value.

Navarra n.v. (Sainsbury's) 11 £B

Utiel Requeña 1988 (Sainsbury's) 12 £B

**Viña Herminia, Luganilla, Riserva Rioja
1985** 13 £D
Either this wine is getting long in the tooth or I am. I find
the ripe quality to the vanilla edging of riojas of any age
rather unsettling. However, once harnessed to good grub,
the wine comes into its own, and this one is excellent with
rice dishes and stews – especially those employing chorizo
sausage. Cooked chorizo and middle-aged rioja make a
splendid pair of cart-horses sufficient to pull the most
jaded of palates out of torpor.

SPANISH WINE – *white*

Blanc de Paraiso n.v.   15   £B
This wine requires a new geographic category to be estab-
lished. It is actually made in France from grapes grown in
Spain. Perhaps not surprisingly, it is effortlessy and
enviably bilingual: it speaks the exuberantly fruity language
of Spain as well as the reluctant acidic tongue of Southern
France. It is almost all fruit, in truth, with a faint undertone
of almond, and it is a wonderful drink merely to glug or to
drink with hors d'oeuvres. It is a gloriously *happy* wine.

La Mancha n.v. (Sainsbury's)   13   £A
Made from the airen which covers so much of Spain that it
makes this grape variety the most extensively planted on
earth. Not surprisingly, therefore, it is a rare A-priced
wine. But this alone does not make it distinctive, for this
example is gently fruity, clean and properly put together. A
winner for heavily attended meetings of the local residents.

Moscatel de Valencia n.v. (Sainsbury's)   14   £B
A huge torrent of toffee, molasses and almonds. Terrific
value for a dessert wine of such oomph. Marvellous with
Christmas pud and cream.

Rioja 1991 (Sainsbury's)   12   £C

Torres Viña Sol 1990   13   £C

Valdepenas Blanc n.v. (Sainsbury's)   15   £B
The airen, picked early from well-sited vineyards on lime-
stone soil, and then lovingly vinified, is no longer the ugly
frog among Spain's grape varieties but a true prince. In this
example the melon/lemon balance, and overall classy feel

make a mockery of airen's rotten reputation, yet, best of all,
is still cheap. Lovely wine, lovely price.

Valencia n.v. (Sainsbury's)　　　　　　12　£A
Just under £2.50 a bottle can't be bad, nor is the wine.
Fresh-faced, barely apple-cheeked, and a mite puny to
finish – but at packed parties who's going to notice anything but the pleasant, clean wine in their glasses?

USA WINE – *red*

**Beaulieu Vineyards Cabernet Sauvignon
1988**　　　　　　　　　　　　　　13　£D
A creamily elegant wine with seductive characteristics.

**California Cabernet Sauvignon n.v.
(Sainsbury's)**　　　　　　　　　　13　£C

La Crema Pinot Noir 1987　　　　　13　£E
By a whisker this wine fails to score even higher. Is it a
failure of the bouquet at the last gasp? A loosening of the
grip of the pinot noir taste as the wine disappears down the
gullet? The wine has class and distinction and its for-
wardness gives it some presence. Yet, in spite of these
qualities, the wine does perhaps need more age to give it
greater complexity and heighten its character.

USA WINE – *white*

California Chardonnay n.v. (Sainsbury's)　　13　£C

Sauvignon Blanc Firestone 1991
(Sainsbury's)   11 £C

Sauvignon Blanc Washington State 1991
(Sainsbury's)   12 £C

SPARKLING WINE/CHAMPAGNE

Australian Sparkling Wine n.v. (Sainsbury's) 15 £D
Apart from *don't*, I can offer the following sound advice to
any individual contemplating marriage: buy this delicious
wine instead of champagne and go somewhere even ritzier
for the honeymoon.

Cava n.v. (Sainsbury's)   14 £C
Simply one of the best cavas around, and many know-
ledgeable drinkers can't tell it from champagne, as I dis-
covered first-hand during the judging of the Sainsbury's/
BBC *Good Food Magazine* Wine Taster of the Year competition.

Champagne Extra Dry n.v. (Sainsbury's)   14 £F
Good at the price; lovely biscuity fruit, and dry with it. So
much better than the famous *marques* for so much less
money.

Crémant d'Alsace, Sparkling n.v.   14 £D
As I write, I receive the news that UK champagne imports
are down 50 per cent on last year. Hopefully, this has a lot
to do with the recession and even more to do with excellent
sparklers like this at half price of the Rheims product. This
particular sparkling wine has a creaminess which will fool
even an experienced boozer.

Crémant de Bourgogne Rosé n.v. (Sainsbury's) 14 £D
Terrific blusher for the money.

Cuvée Napa n.v. 14 £E
This should worry the Champenois sick. True, it's made under Mumm supervision, but its Californian provenance is hard to spot. It's exactly like a *grande marque* brut champagne but at half the price. If I were a sparkling winemaker in Rheims I'd be more nervous than at any time since 1789.

Mercier n.v. 11 £F

Prosecco n.v. (Sainsbury's) 10 £C
On the label, it trumpets itself brassily as 'a quality sparkling wine'. And a brassy beast it is.

Rosé Champagne Brut n.v. (Sainsbury's) 13 £F
Good value at this price and nicely fruity and dry.

Saumur n.v. (Sainsbury's) 14 £D
The bubbles are bursting with pleasant, dry fruit.

Sparkling Vouvray n.v. (Sainsbury's) 14 £D
The smell of the grape, chenin blanc, should be ignored. Concentrate instead on the rounded dryness and suggestion of baked apples.

Vintage Champagne 1986 (Sainsbury's) 14 £F
Excellent value for vintage champagne, but better than the non-vintage? Tough question.

Tesco

ARGENTINIAN WINE – *red*

Cabernet Sauvignon n.v. (Tesco)	11	£B

Trapiche Pinot Noir Reserve 1987　　　　15　£C
A wine which lingers on the palate: rich, properly gamey, good acidic balance, and the whole thing put together very classily.

ARGENTINIAN WINE – *white*

Argentinian White 1991 (Tesco)　　　　11　£B

Trapiche Chardonnay 1990　　　　15　£C
Really quite brilliant value for money for a no-nonsense wine of class, varietal distinction and considerable finesse. Delicious with chicken dishes.

AUSTRALIAN WINE – *red*

Barramundi Shiraz/Merlot n.v.　　　　13　£C
Whacky label, whacky wine. Spicy fruit and calm acid. Good style.

Bin 707 Cabernet Sauvignon, Penfold's 1988　14　£G
Fifteen quid to kiss an Australian? Maybe, but this stuff smacks you in the kisser back.

Cabernet Sauvignon/Shiraz n.v. (Tesco)   15 £C
At this price, a steal. A big mouthful of dry plums and
cherried, spicy prunes. Smashing stuff with real personality.

RF Cabernet Sauvignon 1989   13 £C

Shiraz n.v. (Tesco)   13 £C
The burnt sausage wine *par excellence*.

Yalumba Shiraz 1989   13 £C

AUSTRALIAN WINE – *white*

Australian Chardonnay n.v. (Tesco)   12 £C

Australian Sauvignon Blanc, De Bortoli n.v.
(Tesco)   11 £C

Australian Semillon, De Bortoli n.v. (Tesco) 12 £B

Barramundi Semillon/Chardonnay n.v.   13 £C
Smashing T-shirt label, smashing T-shirt wine. (The fruit
is dressed casually rather than seriously.)

Fumé Blanc, Hunter Valley, Rosemount
1990   12 £D

Houghton Wildflower Ridge Chenin Blanc
1990   13 £C
Some richness of style.

Moondah Brook Verdelho 1990   12 £C

Rhine Riesling n.v.   12 £B

Semillon/Chardonnay 1989, Penfold's   12 £C
Oodles of baked fruit.

AUSTRIAN WINE – *red*

Winzerhaus Blauer Zweigelt 1991   15   £C
As glorious as a summer pudding to behold and (almost) to
taste. Yet it's not sweet but bramble-dry and the crushed
berried fruit has a slight new leather feel to it. Why can't
modern beaujolais be this perfectly alcoholic (11.5 per
cent), this gulpably fruity, and this joyously drinkable?

AUSTRIAN WINE – *white*

Austrian Dry White n.v.   14   £B
Lovely pear, apple and peach fruit and controlled acidity.
Quite delicious and superb value for money.

Winzerhaus Grüner Veltliner 1991   14   £B
Green grass, wet wool, cob nuts and raspberries – now you
know the sort of codswallop wine writers scribble down as
wine notes. In plain English, this means a fully fruity wine
in the mouth with a buttery edge and a good clean finish in
the throat. Excellent value and rather good with codswallop (and most other fish dishes).

Winzerhaus Pinot Blanc 1990   13   £B
Toasty bouquet, slightly sullen fruit. This wine scored a
point higher a year ago. Must be developing in the bottle.
An excellent aperitif or salad wine.

Winzerhaus Welschriesling 1990   13   £B
Only a somewhat short finish prevents this wine from
scoring more. It is pleasant apple and melon production
with merit as an aperitif.

BULGARIAN WINE – *red*

Bulgarian Country Red n.v.   14   £A
A soft, gentle, appealing, simple wine which nevertheless
gushes with blackcurrant fruit from start to finish. It possesses a smoothness which is good value for under £2.50.
Dusty floorboards and old leather to smell. Sweet fruit to
swallow. Rather good with a rich meat stew or bread and
blue cheese.

Melnik Reserve 1984   13   £C
Doesn't muck about for a second – it clouts you in the
kisser with ripe fruit, grabs the teeth and won't let go.

BULGARIAN WINE – *white*

Bulgarian Country White n.v.   14   £A
Very clean, no overpowering richness of fruit, but good
balance and some style. Good value.

CHILEAN WINE – *red*

Chilean Cabernet Sauvignon n.v. (Tesco)   14   £B
Chewy, oaky, lots of toothsome dried fruit. Terrific value.

Cousino Macul, Merlot 1988   15   £C
Ripe and curranty, this is a most approachable merlot with
no trace of the stalkiness which often distinguishes this
grape variety. Lovely big chocolate and dry, soft molasses

feel in the mouth. Tremendously gluggable. Great company with a book.

Merlot 1990 (Tesco) 14 £B
Great value from the Santa Rita vineyard. Soft yet gently stalky and deliberately understated fruitiness.

Montes Alpha Cabernet Sauvignon 1987 15 £E
Behind a label giving the impression of an Edwardian funeral invitation skulks an astounding mish-mash of pungent blackcurrant, mint and chocolate. This sounds like an After Eight confection but it is in fact a wine of such gorgeously deep velvety fruitiness that the taste-buds cower in bruised surprise then come back crying 'More! More! More!'

CHILEAN WINE – *white*

Chardonnay 1991 (Tesco) 13 £C

Sauvignon Blanc, Santa Rita 1991 14 £B
An accurate stab at elegance and class for a bargain price.

Villard Chardonnay 1990 12 £C

Villard Sauvignon Blanc 1991 11 £C

CHINESE WINE – *white*

Tsingtao Chardonnay 1988 12 £D
This vintage is getting on a bit. Tesco's will be auctioning it at Sotheby's soon.

CYPRIOT WINE – *red*

Cyprus Red, Keo n.v. (Tesco)   4 £B
Bought by nostalgia seekers thirsty for memories of the
country they've left behind, this wine is nigh-undrinkable.
Good basis for a whacky vinaigrette. Is it fortified? Its
drinkers need to be. (And these drinkers exist. The store
sells 60,000 bottles a year!)

CYPRIOT WINE – *white*

Keo   11 £B

FRENCH WINE – *red*

Beaujolais n.v. (Tesco)   10 £C

Bourgueil, Domaine Hubert, La Huralaie
1990   15 £D
This red Loire wine with its slatey, raspberry taste is
outstanding, and this '90 vintage is considerably more
toothsome than the previous one. Rich and dry, this wine is
beautiful with all barbecued meats and grilled or roast
vegetables with haloumi cheese and herbs sprinkled over.

Burgundy, Henri de Bahezre n.v. (Tesco)   12 £C

Buzet, Domaine de la Croix 1988   12 £C
Hairy-bottomed maturity with this wine. Very good with
roast food and sausages.

**Cabernet Sauvignon, Haute Vallée de l'Aude n.v.
(Tesco)**　　　　　　　　　　　　13　£B
Excellent value for the family get-together with a roast on
the table.

Château Bois Galant, Médoc 1986　　　　13　£D
Quite distinguished in its own way and reasonably complex. It cries out for food as Romeo cries out for Juliet.

Château Cantemerle, Haut-Médoc 1987　　13　£F

Château d'Arsac, Haut-Médoc 1988　　　12　£D

Château de Camensac, Haut-Médoc 1988　13　£E

Château de Caraguilhes 1988　　　　　14　£C
The well-stacked organic wine from Corbières, an area
transitionally replacing Beaujolais as the area for highly
drinkable cheap red wines. This tastes nothing like beaujolais, thank goodness, but comes across as earthily
natural, rich, and deeply satisfying.

**Château des Gondats, Bordeaux Supérieur
1989**　　　　　　　　　　　　　　13　£C

**Château du Bluizard, Beaujolais Villages
1990**　　　　　　　　　　　　　　12　£C
In spite of the back label claiming that this wine's maker,
Jean de St-Charle, is world-famous, his eminence has,
until now, failed to penetrate the closed clam I must
inhabit. His wine is okay with egg and chips.

**Château Léon, Premières Côtes de Bordeaux
1987**　　　　　　　　　　　　　　12　£C

Château Les Gravières, St-Emilion 1988　14　£E
Delicious, soft, very supple.

Château Marquis-de-Terme, Margaux 1987   14   £E
Big, chewy, with well-developed fruit. Tarry aroma. Very
oily and sinuous on the palate. A touch grand.

**Château Pigoudet, Coteaux d'Aix-en-Provence
1988   14   £C**
Sunny (and pretty) Provence in a bottle, plus a touch of
Côtes-du-Rhône earthiness. Excellent drinking.

Château St-Georges, St-Emilion 1986   13   £G

Château St-Nicholas, Fronsac 1987   10   £D

Château Toutigeac 1989   13   £C
An excellent dry fruity wine firmly in the Bordeaux style.
Good for serious dinner parties and roast beef (if there is
anyone left in the land who still does such things).

Châteauneuf-du-Pape, Les Arnevels 1990   14   £D
Meaty, rich, well-muscled. A classy dollop of fruit.

Chinon, Baronnies Madeleine 1983   15   £D
Rare to find a Chinon of such age on a supermarket shelf.
Curiously, the wine seemed in its dotage a year or so ago,
but a transformation has taken place and the old dog has
been taught several new tricks. It comes up still smelling of
old carpets and tar, but the dried raspberries are more in
evidence, and now it seems a perfectly rounded specimen
of great charm.

Claret, Yvon Mau n.v. (Tesco)   14   £B
One of the finest examples of cheap bordeaux on sale – the
typical grassy tannins and fruit are tremendous with roast
foods. But this is not a wine of a particular year, so I feel
obliged to point out that the secret of the consistent excellence is to be found in the blending of various wines, and if
these wines are not available, or newer vintages of them are

different in style, then one batch of Tesco claret will be different from another. That said, this wine has never let me down yet.

Clos de Chenoves, Bourgogne, Buxy 1988   13 £D
This is no bad red burgundy for the money. (Especially when so many cost an arm and a leg and aren't worth the grit under your little finger-nail.)

Côte Rôtie, Michel Bernard 1989   13 £E

Côtes de Duras 1989   11 £B

Côtes du Frontonnais 1988   13 £B

Côtes du Rhône n.v. (Tesco)   12 £B

Côtes du Rhône Villages 1990   13 £C

Domaine Beaulieu St-Saveur, Marmandais 1990   12 £B
A writer's wine. Has ink on the fruit.

Domaine de Beaufort, Minervois 1990   14 £B
Sweet cloves; amazing ripe, teeth-embracing, soft, spicy fruit. Great value.

Domaine de Conroy, Brouilly 1990   11 £D

Domaine des Baumelles, Côtes du Luberon 1990   13 £C

Domaine Les Hauts des Chambert, Cahors 1986   13 £D
Good bit of bottle-age does wonders for the right wine.

Dorgan, Vin de Pays de l'Aude n.v. (Tesco)   14 £B
Slightly peppery wine of excellent firm structure and attractive fruitiness.

Escoubes, Côtes de Gascogne n.v. (Tesco)   12   £B

Fitou n.v. (Tesco)   11   £B

French Country Cabernet Sauvignon n.v. (Tesco)
(1 litre)   12   £B

French Country Red n.v. (Tesco) (1 litre)   14   £B
Utterly straightforward drinkable plonk which is as soft and
attractive on the fruit as it is soft and attractive on the wallet.
That litre works out at under 40p a glass.

Gevrey Chambertin, Marchand 1988   13   £F

Grand Carat 1990   8   £B
Smells of potatoes, tastes of old socks. Maybe it's actually
made from grand carats.

Hautes Côtes de Nuits, Caves des Hautes Côtes
1988   13   £D

Hautes Côtes du Beaune, Caves des Hautes Côtes
1989   13   £D

Hermitage, Domaine Cécile Mussel 1988   11   £F

La Vieille Ferme Reserve, Côtes du Rhône
1990   16   £C
This is a branded wine but it is usually a Côtes du Ventoux
not a Côtes du Rhone. Either way, La Vieille Ferme doesn't
exist as a vineyard; it is merely a vehicle for its owner, M.
Perrin (who has risen and risen ever since he created it), to
carry any wine he likes. However, this reserve wine is easily
the best branded red wine I have ever tasted. It liberally
coats the tongue in lashings of soft fruit to give the feel of
crystallized velvet. A masterpiece of blending.

Les Forts de Latour, Pauillac 1982   10   £H
Blimey! Wot a lot of dosh!

| Les Terres Fines, Syrah 1989 | 10 | £B |

| Margaux 1988 (Tesco) | 11 | £E |

| Médoc n.v. (Tesco) | 11 | £C |

Merlot n.v. (Tesco) 13 £B
Bargain – especially if you hanker after grass and green peppercorns with your fruit.

| Morgon, Arthur Barolet 1989 | 12 | £D |

| Pauillac 1987 (Tesco) | 10 | £D |

| Pavillon Rouge du Château Margaux 1989 | 12 | £G |

| Saumur Champigny 1986 | 13 | £D |

Savigny les Beaune, Hospices de Beaune
1986 12 £F

| St-Emilion n.v. (Tesco) | 12 | £C |

| St-Joseph 1989 | 10 | £C |

Syrah, Vin de Pays des Collines Rhondaniennes
n.v. 13 £B

Vin de Pays des Coteaux de la Cité de Carcassonne
1990 12 £B

Vin de Pays des Côtes de Gascogne, Yvon Mau
n.v. 11 £A

FRENCH WINE – *white*

| Alsace Gewürztraminer 1990 (Tesco) | 10 | £C |

Alsace Pinot Blanc n.v. (Tesco)	10	£B
Alsace Riesling 1990 (Tesco)	11	£C
Beaujolais Blanc 1990	12	£C
Blayais n.v.	10	£B

Cabernet de Saumur, Caves des Vignerons de Saumur, Rosé 1990   13   £B

Cépage Terret, Vin de Pays de l'Hérault, Delta Domaines 1990 and 1991   13   £B
Good balance, good price, good by itself.

Chablis, Bacheroy-Josselin 1991   11   £C

Chablis, La Chablisienne 1990 (Tesco)   12   £D

Chablis Premier Cru, Montmain, La Chablisienne 1988   12   £E

Château de Carles Sauternes 1989   12   £F
Yes, it's a lot of dosh, but it's a lot of posh – a fine, full sauternes with all the honey, molasses (burnt) and creamy fruit you could wish for. But is it four times better than Tesco's Moscatel de Valencia? Only if a real aficionado is coming to dinner and you must seduce him or her at all costs.

Château La Forêt St-Hilaire, Entre-Deux-Mers 1990   12   £C

Château Le Gay, Bordeaux 1989   11   £C

Château Les Girotins, Sauternes 1989 (half)   13   £D
Luscious pudding wine, in a handy helping (exclusive to Tesco) with all the honeyed effect you could wish for. Delightful.

Château Magneau, Graves 1989   14   £E

A gorgeous, smoky, woody, raspberry-ringed, clean wine which even at this price makes you rejoice and throw all your worries out the window. A lovely mouthful.

Château Malagar, Bordeaux Blanc 1990   15   £C

This wine claims, rather pompously, to be an ancient property of François Mauriac, who picked up the Nobel Prize for Literature in 1952. You might with equal pretension urge a man to watch Tottenham Hotspur on the premise that the club once enjoyed the support of Freddie Ayer. Let not this affectation deter you from sampling this wine's fascinating blend of firm, rather prim fruit, graceful balancing acidity and subtle nuttiness. It is supremely drinkable, with the deep aromatic seriousness and multi-textured body of a wine costing a deal more.

Château Vert Bois 1990   13   £C

A refreshing little wine made, appropriately, by a man called tea. Lovely rich aroma and a bit of decent fruit.

Châteauneuf-du-Pape, Les Arnevels, Quiot
1990   14   £D

White Châteauneuf-du-Pape is not to everyone's taste, with its curious soft, slightly creamy, very dry style, but this example begs to be tried. It is a lovely wine, dry yet cheekily fruity, with a gorgeous underlying acidity.

Domaine de Collin Rozier, Chardonnay, Vin de Pays d'Oc 1989   13   £D

Domaine de Jalousie, Late Harvest 1989,
Grassa   12   £C

A very engaging pre-prandial tipple. The touch of treacle on the fruit (while, paradoxically, clean) is quite pleasant. But as a dessert wine forget it.

Domaine de la Jalousie, Cuvée Bois, 1989   13   £C
Happy integration of wood and fruit. And no overdosing of the latter, either. A charming little wine.

Domaine St-Alain, Vin de Pays des Côtes du Tarn n.v.   11   £B

Dry Muscat, Vin de Pays d'Oc 1991 (Tesco)   13   £B
A pleasant aperitif.

Entre-Deux-Mers n.v. (Tesco)   12   £B

Escoubes, Vin de Pays des Côtes de Gascogne 1990 (Tesco)   12   £B
Smells like an old rain-soaked jumper drying off in front of the fire, but this woolliness masks a clean taste with an agreeable amount of ripe, melony fruit leading up to a sharpish finish.

Floc de Gascogne n.v.   14   £D
This is a curiosity. It is 17 per cent alcohol, made with fresh grape juice with a dash of armagnac, and it is very sweet. But it is also a pleasant, tough, peasant aperitif, and I enjoy it.

French Chardonnay de l'Aude n.v. (Tesco)   10   £B

French Country White n.v. (Tesco) (1 litre)   13   £C
A Côtes de Gascogne in origin but with none of the booming fruit – instead the pineapples and peaches and lemons combine most happily to make a happy little wine. Excellent value.

French Country White, Côtes de Gascogne n.v. (Tesco)   13   £C
You get a litre of dry, clean yet melony wine for the money which works out at 45p a glass.

Graves, Yvon Mau n.v. (Tesco) 11 £C

Les Terres Fines, Muscat Sec 1990 12 £C
A summer garden aperitif rather than a dessert wine. I
suppose you could drink it in the house with the central
heating on full blast.

Mâcon Blanc Villages 1990 (Tesco) 11 £C

**Menetou-Salon, Domaine de la Montaloise
1989** 12 £C

Miribeau, Vin de Pays d'Oc sur Lie 1991 12 £B

Monbazillac n.v. (Tesco) 12 £C

**Muscadet Sur Lie, Domaine de la Huperie
1990** 12 £C

Muscat, Cuvée Jose Sala n.v. 15 £B
There are few such honey-toffeed dessert wines around at
this price. Not as deep and as rich as a pricier Beaumes de
Venise or first-growth sauternes, but what do you expect
for such a small amount?

Pouilly Fumé, Cuvée Jules 1990 11 £D
Would be excellent value at £3.25, but at nigh on seven
quid its lack of weight tells against it.

Premières Côtes de Bordeaux n.v. (Tesco) 11 £B

Sancerre, Alphonse Mellot 1990 11 £E

Sauvignon Blanc, Bordeaux n.v. (Tesco) 13 £B
Excellent value – dry, clean and melony fruity.

St-Romain Blanc, Arthur Barolet 1988 13 £E
Some reasonably attractive woody fruit here.

Vin de Pays de la Dordogne, Sigoules n.v.   12   £B

**Vin de Pays des Coteaux des Baronnies, Chardonnay
1990**   11   £B
Those des's don't add up to a des. res. as far as the fruit is
concerned. If it's at home, it doesn't answer the door. Still,
you can't grumble with the freshness of the wine or the
price.

Vin de Pays des Côtes du Tarn n.v.   11   £B
Old woolly socks and tangy fruit.

GERMAN WINE – *red*

Baden Pinot Noir 1990   12   £C
Dry and rather reminiscent of strawberry cough-sweets.
Rather appealing in an incongruous, cheeky sort of way,
like a beggar in a fox fur coat.

GERMAN WINE – *white*

Baden Dry n.v.   12   £B
Sound value to be had here. Stale cooked string-beans,
slight touch of spice, keen fruit.

Bereich Johannisberg Riesling, Krayer 1989   11   £B

Bernkasteler Kurfurstlay n.v.   13   £B
Great-value riesling with a freshness and a fruity steeliness
which will handsomely partner a rich crab salad.

Brauneberger Kurfurstlay Riesling Kabinett
1990   12   £C
Delicious aperitif: fragrant, light and not too sweet.

Grans Fassian, Riesling Trocken 1990   13   £D
A great, great aperitif tipple: rose-water, lemons and citric
toffee. Huge acidity cloaking it all.

Guldentaler Auslese n.v.   14   £C
Great smell of lemon and eau de cologne. Searing fruit
dipped in acid, nervous lemon finish. A classic riesling
assault on the senses which a plate of smoked eel with
horseradish will make marvellous sense of.

Hock n.v. (Tesco)   11   £A

Johannisberger Klaus Riesling, Schloss Schönborn
1989   11   £C

Kreuznacher Narrenkappe, Riesling Auslese,
Anheuser 1976   14   £F
Imagine cream, honey and nuts liquidized and left for
yonks to blend brilliantly. This wine is all that in a glass.
Lovely with pud, with ice-cream even (legendarily, an
impossible partner for wine) or fresh fruit.

Morio Muskat n.v.   12   £B
Good grapey aperitif.

Mosel Medium Dry Riesling n.v. (Tesco)   11   £B

Niersteiner Gutes Domtal n.v.   12   £A

Niersteiner Pettenthal Riesling Spätlese Balbach
1985   11   £D

**Piesporter Treppchen Riesling Kabinett
1990**   12 £C
Pre-prandial Piesporter.

**Rauenthaler Rothenberg, Riesling Kabinett
1988**   11 £C

**Rauenthaler Rothenberg, Riesling Spätlese
1988**   11 £D

Rheinpfalz Dry Riesling n.v.   12 £B
Chilled, in the garden, as a taste-bud tickler, this wine is
fine. Or try it with sparkling mineral water as a spritzer.

Rheinpfalz Medium Dry Silvaner n.v.   11 £B

Ruppertsberger Hoheberg, Riesling 1987   13 £C
This is a halbtrocken wine, which means it is half-dry.
This does not mean, though, that the other half is sweet.
On the contrary, this wine has the muscular elegance to be
most acceptable with a Sunday lunch of roast pork with
apple sauce.

Saar Tafelwein n.v. (Tesco)   12 £A
At under £2.50 this is an agreeable aperitif with its melony
aroma and aftertaste; or, with its pleasant medium-bodied
style, good with food for those who dislike bone-dry
whites.

Scharzhofberger Van Volxem 1990   13 £C
A delicious, silky, lemon-sherbert aperitif.

**Steinweiler Kloster Liebfrauenberg Auslese n.v.
(Tesco)**   12 £C

**Steinweiler Kloster Liebfrauenberg Kabinett n.v.
(Tesco)**   10 £B

Steinweiler Kloster Liebfrauenberg Spâtlese n.v. (Tesco) 11 £C

Stettener Stein, Franken n.v. 11 £C
Vigorous, appley, dry wine of interest to oyster lovers. The bottle makes a handsome lampshade when empty (or even full if you like to live dangerously).

St-Joanner Abtei Auslese n.v. (Tesco) 13 £C

St-Johanner Abtei Kabinett n.v. (Tesco) 11 £B

St-Johanner Abtei Spätlese n.v. (Tesco) 12 £B
Nice with a fresh, crisp apple and a chunk of cheese.

Trittenheimer Altarchen, Riesling 1989 12 £C

Villa Stock Halbtrocken, Riesling n.v. 12 £B
Good with fish soup.

Weissburgunder 1989 12 £C

GREEK WINE – *red*

Nemea 1989 12 £C

GREEK WINE – *white*

Kretikos 1990 12 £C

HUNGARIAN WINE – *white*

Hungarian Chardonnay 1989 (Tesco)   10   £B

ITALIAN WINE – *red*

Barbaresco 1986 (Tesco)   13   £D

Barbera, Valle de Sole 1987   14   £E
Hints of fig and rose-water make this a fine mouthful. Dry,
excellently balanced.

Barolo, Giacosa Fratelli 1986   13   £D

Barolo, Riserva Chiarlo 1982   13   £F
A lot of money for a lot of wine. But a cool-headed barolo
for all that. None of those sweaty, hairy armpits swimming
with liquorice as with many a barolo – just pleasant fruit
and firmly herbal undertones.

Briccoviole, Sebaste 1987   13   £E
Stylish fruitwise and interestingly creamy. Don't let the
humble Vino da Tavola designation put you off. This wine,
made from a highly individual blend of nebbiolo and barbera grape varieties, offends Italian wine laws. It can't call
itself barolo for a start, even though it is made there.

Cabernet Sauvignon, Ca Donini 1989   13   £C
No sour grapes with this Italian copy of a French masterpiece; just lots of fruit, masses of quaffability, and tons of
value.

Carmignano 1987   16   £D
The plainest, most elegant calling-card of a label. A most
distinguished aroma of cooked figs and beautiful, clean
fruit (blackcurrant and raspberry) and a firm finish. Superb
classy wine from Capezzana, an island and a law unto itself
amidst the great sea of chianti which surrounds it. This
wine will improve in bottle, too, in spite of its eminent
drinkability now. A bargain under £6.

Chianti 1989 (Tesco)   15   £B
Easily one of the best chiantis around for the brilliant value
for money it represents. An immediately attractive and very
drinkable wine with lots of fruit and Tuscan earthiness. It
is around 6op cheaper than the supposed superior Classico
below and it ought to be less good, but it isn't.

Chianti Classico 1989 (Tesco)   14   £B
Soft in a hairy-chested sort of way – husky-voiced and
floral. Baked earth fruit and herbs. Lush with softness yet
acidic freshness. Smashing.

Chianti Classico, Monte Firidolfi 1988   14   £C
Woody, husky, fruity.

Chianti Rufina, Grati 1989   14   £B
Delicious dry stuff – an exceptional chianti for the money.
Has all the gruff-mannered elegance of the type and it
seems to reek of terracotta fruitiness.

Chianti Rufina, Villa di Monte 1985   11   £C

Copertino 1988   15   £B
Dry, rich and very velvety. Utterly seductive with pasta and
bacon bits.

Merlot del Piave n.v.   11   £B

Montepulciano d'Abruzzo, Bianchi 1990   14   £B
Just the colour of this wine sets my teeth tingling. It has a
good acidic spine to a nicely developed, fruity body, and
with pastas with tomato or basil sauces it is perfection.

Montepulciano d'Abruzzo, Villa Paola 1987   13   £C
Gorgeous, gooey stuff for two passionate, but as yet
unconnected, would-be lovers to become mellow about
whilst consuming spaghetti with bacon and garlic.

Montelpulciano d'Abruzzo, Villa Torre 1990   15   £B
Excellent value for a ravishing little tart of ample charms.
Fruity, dry; rotting berries to smell and taste. Superb solo
bottle or with pasta and pesto sauce.

Orfeno dell'Uccellina 1990   13   £C

Pinot Noir del Veneto (Tesco)   12   £B
Rich little aroma, fresh raspberry acid. Cool it and enjoy.

Recioto della Valpolicella 1985   14   £D
This is made from semi-dried grapes and it shows in a
distinguished, curranty wine which is all-embracingly
fruity yet dry. Marvellous with stews and roasts which
feature dried fruits, but especially toothsome with rich
cheeses (blue and goat's).

Ripa della Mandorle 1986   15   £D
The elegance! Made by an Englishman in Greve, what's
more. Unlike some of the wonderful fat peasants above
with their coarse manners and feverish fruitness, John
Matta's ripa is classy, dry and very serious, with a long,
earthy finish and quietly understated liquorice charm. A
soothing wine.

Rosso Rubino 1988   13   £B

Sicilian Red n.v. (Tesco) 14 £B

A fruity, spirited little thing with a finish recalling the smell of Ferrari tyres rising off the autostrada. Nice warm rubbery mouthful of fruit. A smashing wine to enjoy with lots of friends and masses of pasta dripping with garlic.

Tesco Dolcetto d'Acqui 1990 15 £B

Mouth-wateringly good value. A delicious, sweet-natured, cheering wine of soothing acidity and lovely gushing fruit, arm-flinging and expressive. Yummy.

Valle del Sole Barbera, Gallo d'Oro 1987 12 £E

Villa di Monte, Chianti Rufina Reserva 1979 11 £D

Chianti this mature does not grow on trees and there is barely a year of life left in this particular example. It seems to have lost the exuberance and freshness of youth and wilted to a rather unremarkable and tired old age. Nevertheless, it would partner spaghetti carbonara without disgracing itself.

ITALIAN WINE – *white*

Bianco d'Alcamo 1990 13 £C

Lemonic, balanced, fresh, and excellent with fish dishes.

Chardonnay, Alto Adige, E. Von Keller 1990 15 £C

Perfect wine, perfectly priced. Lovely graceful entrance of the fruit hand-in-hand with the acidity, like two angels. A master class in simple chardonnay-making at a reasonable sum.

Chardonnay del Veneto n.v. (Tesco) 13 £B

Bright fruit, fair acid, reasonable balance. Performs well for the money.

Colli Albani, Cantina Sociale 1990 (Tesco)   12   £B
Good value.

Frascati n.v. (Tesco)   13   £B

Gambellara, Monte Bocara 1990   13   £C
The feeble bouquet apart, this is quite classy wine in other
departments, with a good weight of rich fruit and firm
freshness.

Locorotondo n.v.   12   £B
Spicy aroma, nutty and sour melon fruit.

Montepulciano Cerasulo 1990 (Rosé)   13   £C

Naragus 1990   14   £B
Still a terrific Sardinian winner, this wine. Offers great
freshness of style with underlying soft fruitiness.

Orvieto Classico, Vaselli 1990   12   £B

Pinot Grigio del Veneto, Vino da Tavola 1989
(Tesco)   13   £C

Pinot Grigio, Tiefenbrunner 1990   13   £C

Sicilian White n.v. (Tesco)   13   £B
A bargain of a drinkable wine for slurping in vast quantities
by itself or with pasta and seafood dishes.

Soave Classico n.v. (Tesco)   12   £B

Terre di Ginestra 1990   13   £C
Grown in bandit country (i.e. in Sicily) from a single
honest grape variety, the cataratto. Under a toothy, fruity
cloak it hides a steely touch.

**Terre Toscano, Cantina del Vini Tipici 1990
(Tesco)** 13 £B
Nice prickle with this one.

Verdicchio dei Castelli di Jesi Classico 1991 13 £C
Sponge-cake smell plus a great fight between the fruit
(raspberry and apple) as to which has the upper hand, and
then in comes a subtle bitter finish.

Verdicchio, Villa Bianchi 1990 12 £C

MEXICAN WINE – *red*

Cabernet Sauvignon 1987 (Tesco) 14 £C
Fine style from L. A. Cetto. Brunt toffeed fruit (plum and
blackberry). Well-balanced, well-structured.

**L. A. Cetto Mexican Cabernet Sauvignon
1985** 14 £C
How well would this wine shift if it said Baja California
instead of Mexico on the label, as legitimately it could? A
creamy, elegant wine of substance and class.

NEW ZEALAND WINE – *red*

Cabernet/Merlot 1989 (Tesco) 14 £C
Excellent behaviour, excellent balance, excellent style. If
that sounds like a school report on an outstanding gymnast,
so be it. This wine has text-book qualities.

Timara Cabernet Sauvignon/Merlot n.v. 11 £C

NEW ZEALAND WINE – *white*

New Zealand Sauvignon Blanc 1991 (Tesco)   13   £C
With sauvignon blanc fast treading on the heels of chardonnay as *the* international white wine, interesting examples are not as common as you might think. But this is a pleasant exception and does manage to make the fruit palatable, with no screaming tinned-pineapple flavouring, and the acidity personable.

Sauvignon Blanc 1991 (Tesco)   12   £C
Spring flowers and cabbages.

Sauvignon Blanc, Nobilo 1990   10   £D

Stoneleigh Chardonnay 1990   12   £D

Timara Chardonnay/Semillon 1990   12   £C

PORTUGUESE WINE – *red*

Bairrada 1987 (Tesco)   13   £B

Borba 1989   14   £B
Lots of zingy fruit and great thrusting style. If you can imagine chewing a hot terracotta roof-tile and blackcurrant crumble baked with all-spice, you get some idea of this wine's approach.

Casa Portuguesa n.v.   14   £B
An excellent raspberry-scented, lightly woody wine.

Dão 1987 (Tesco)   13   £B
Velvety fruit, worth investing in at this price.

Dom Jose n.v. 14 £A
A marvellous food-wine – ripe, randy, saucy and as
sweatily old-fashioned as Fielding's Tom Jones. Don't
think of drinking it until at least an hour (maybe two or
three) has passed after opening it. It needs air to develop
and food to live.

Douro 1985 (Tesco) 13 £B

Periquita 1989 14 £A
Great value for great fresh fruit.

Quinta da Cardiga n.v. 13 £A
Bargain sausage-and-mash red.

Tinto Velho 1986 14 £C
Leather, herbs and dried raspberries. Quite a recipe.
Great with herb-drenched grilled meat.

PORTUGUESE WINE – *white*

Bairrada 1990 (Tesco) 14 £B
Really. Under three quid this wine is scandalously under-
priced. As the final ingredient in a fish stew or mushroom
risotto or grilled lemon chicken meal, it is superb.

Casa Portuguesa White n.v. 11 £B

Dry Portuguese Rosé n.v. 12 £B

João Pires Moscato 1990 14 £C
A gorgeous, lanky wine of dryness yet freshness. A perfect
muscat aperitif.

SOUTH AFRICAN WINE – *red*

Cabernet Sauvignon, Kloof-en-Dal 1987	11	£C
Pinotage, Paarl 1989	12	£B

SOUTH AFRICAN WINE – *white*

Boschendal, Paarl 1990   10   £E

Chardonnay, Kloof-en-Dal 1990   10   £C

Colombar 1991   12   £B
German on the nose, Australian on the palate, English in
the throat. This is, however, a very subtle identity-crisis.

Danie de Wet Chardonnay 1991   13   £C
Individual. Nice and very fresh-finishing, with a subtle
weight of fruit.

Goiya Kgelisje 1992   11   £B
Oh, I wish I could like this wine more! It's a splendid
initiative: 1. It was the first 1992 wine on sale in the UK. 2.
Its name in Kung – the language of the bushmen of the
region – tickles my fancy as does the grotesque neon label.
3. It is a sauvignon blanc of freshness and pear-drop
fruitiness.

La Bri Sauvignon Blanc 1990   12   £C

Van Loveren Pinot Gris 1991   10   £C
Tough to rate this wine without the feeling that I do it an
injustice. It is not cheap for a start. It is also highly

alcoholic and a sourpuss of a wine, with grassy and wet earth undertones which do not endear it to me, but others may find these features adorable.

SPANISH WINE – *red*

Ardal, Ribera del Duero 1990 13 £B
Lovely aubergine colour and excellent to drink with vegetables grilled with cheese. Grips the teeth, this wine, with dried fruit. Good price.

Camporocal, Somontano 1990 12 £B
Great value.

Conde Bravo 1990 12 £C
Wine from the Costa Brava. (They had to turn their hand to something, with all those tourists gone.)

Don Darias n.v. 12 £A

Gran Don Darias n.v. 13 £B

Rioja n.v. (Tesco) 13 £C
Delicious, controlled rioja in a lighter vein than the hot-blooded vanilla-flavoured variety we've learned to loathe. Pretty wine.

Rioja Reserva 1983 (Tesco) 13 £D
In spite of a slight overkill of vanilla from the oak-ageing, a firm, fruity specimen. It yells out for food to be consumed with it.

**Señorio de Guadianeja, Cabernet Sauvignon,
Gran Reserva 1983**   12 £D
A smell of sherry vanilla and a taste of blackcurrant sorbet.
Interesting.

Señorio de los Llanos 1984   15 £C
A terrific satiny, supple, fruity wine of great style and
mature classiness. Thought-provoking (how do they do it
for the money?) and very good with rich spicy dishes.

Toro 1989   13 £C
A hefty mouthful of blackberries and currants. Good value.

Viña del Castillo 1990   15 £B
Outstanding value. Fabulously fruity, all-embracing
combo of strawberries and blackcurrants, cut with excellent acidity. Under £3, a remarkable dollop of plonk.

Viña San Jose 1988   15 £C
An interesting multi-layered Penedes wine with three distinct sides to its impressive personality: 1. root vegetables
to smell; 2. mature fruit to taste, nicely dry, with a touch of
chocolate; 3. almonds going down the throat – very subtle.

SPANISH WINE – *white*

Calverol Blancs de Blancs 1990   13 £B
Clean, fruity (melon), and gently acidic. Great value.

Camporocal, Somontano 1990   13 £B
Good value. Terrific fruit/acid balance.

Cautro Rayas, Rueda 1990   10 £B

Don Darias n.v.　12　£A

Huelva n.v. (Tesco)　12　£B
Great value.

Moscatel de Valencia n.v. (Tesco)　15　£B
If there is such a thing as a peasant dessert wine, this is it.
So rich it would overpower dessert grapes, but not bread
and butter pud. (Try this wine with that very British afters
just once and, I promise, you'll kill to get seconds.)

Rioja n.v. (Tesco)　13　£C
Among the most restrained and courtly of white riojas, this
one. The vanilla-and-banana fruitiness performs in a
nicely understated way. Good with a mild fish curry.

Viña Amalia 1990　12　£B

Viña del Castillo 1990　12　£B

USA WINE – *red*

Californian Red n.v. (Tesco)　13　£B
Interesting what went through the label designer's mind
when (s)he designed this curious blue and somewhat
incongruous townscape on the bottle. Maybe too much of
this wine perhaps? Very audacious. The wine only sur-
prises by being soft and dry and quiet-mannered.

Jack London Cabernet Sauvignon 1987　12　£F
I don't know about White Fang. Feed him a bowl of this
wine and it would be Black Fang.

ZD Pinot Noir Napa Valley 1986　11　£F

USA WINE – *white*

Californian White n.v. (Tesco)	12 £C

Light, floral, very pleasant.

SPARKLING WINE/CHAMPAGNE

Asti Spumante (Tesco) 10   £C

Australian Sparkling Brut n.v. (Tesco) 15   £C
Under a fiver it's one of the best-value sparkling wines on sale. Dry yet nicely edged with fruit.

Blanc de Blancs Champagne n.v. (Tesco) 12   £A

Cava n.v. (Tesco) 13   £C

Champagne n.v. (Tesco) 13   £F
Very good value; even at this modestly respectable score it is better than most big *marques* – dry, with a good acid balance.

Chardonnay Frizzante n.v. 10   £B

Chardonnay Spumante n.v. 15   £D
Great-value sparkler with a great touch of Italian bravura on the typical chardonnay fruit.

Crémant de Bourgogne, Vire 1989 (Tesco) 14   £D
The slightly earthy edge to the fruit is most attractive. The price is even better.

Crémant de Loire Rosé, Cave des Vignerons de Saumur n.v. 12   £D

Deutz, New Zealand n.v. 12 £F
Just like Deutz champagne from the well-known Rheims company.

**Grand Duchess Brut Sparkling Wine, Russia
n.v.** 10 £C
Made near Odessa, the Blackpool of Russia, for all those Siberian miners on their annual hols.

Henri Mandois/Champagne n.v. 12 £F

Lindauer Brut n.v. 12 £D

Michel Arnould Champagne n.v. 12 £G

Moscato d'Asti Gallo d'Oro 1989 13 £C
A great peachy, pear-like sparkling wine, which is marvellous with pud.

Niersteiner Gutes Domtal n.v. (Tesco) 11 £D

Salinger 1988 12 £D
Whizz fizz from Oz at a cheap champagne price.

Soave Classico Spumante DOC n.v. 13 £D
Made to sip with almonds, a glass of this before dinner is a brilliant idea. (And the brain-dead among your guests will say, 'I like this champagne.')

**Sparkling Chardonnay, Louis Changarnier
n.v.** 14 £C
True, I've smelt water with more character to its bouquet, but let not this blemish put you off. The delightful fruit and acid in the mouth and a sunniness of disposition only to be expected of a wine made in Provence, compensate for this as does the reasonable weight of finish. Would do well at a coming-of-age party.

Vintage Champagne Premier Cru 1983
(Tesco)   11   £G

Waitrose

ARGENTINIAN WINE – *red*

Trapiche Malbec 1988   13   £B
Very good-value, stylish wine made from the grape variety
which, in minute quantities, appears in many a Bordeaux
château's wine.

AUSTRALIAN WINE – *red*

Coldridge Estate Cabernet Sauvignon 1990   13   £C

Lachland Springs Cabernet/Shiraz n.v.   14   £B
What a great big hairy-chested bargain we have here. Nice
boot-polish and old-socks aroma leading to a figgy fruitiness of great dryness. Leading contender for the most
off-putting label of the year.

Leasingham Domaine Shiraz 1989   13   £C
They must use the scrapings from a kangaroo's pouch to
give this wine its glorious, spicy, pungent leather character.
Smashing stuff for barbecued foods.

Hardy's Southern Creek Shiraz/Cabernet
1991   12   £C

Koonunga Hill Shiraz/Cabernet 1989   14   £C
Despite approaching the fiver price-tag (of which I

disapprove), this wine is one of the smoothest shiraz/
cabernet marriages to come out of Oz.

Leasingham Domaine Shiraz 1989   14   £C
Delicious, complex, dry – superb with grilled chops.

Penfold's Bin 35 Shiraz/Cabernet 1990   14   £C
Big, bruising fruit in the usual Aussie style. Good value,
too, in this bottle.

AUSTRALIAN WINE – *white*

Hardy's Early Bird 1991   13   £C

Hardy's Southern Creek Semilion/Chardonnay
1991   13   £C

Hill-Smith Old Triangle Riesling 1991   15   £C
A touch of unctuosity on the fruit and a great tangy acidity
make a terrific wine to enjoy by itself with a Ruth Rendell
mystery. Though the wine may provide the greater mystery
as you ask yourself how they do it for under four quid.

Koonunga Hill Chardonnay 1991   14   £C
Oh, I do wish these Penfold's wines wouldn't skirt so close
to a fiver. All the same, this is glorious fruity guzzling.

Mitchelton Sauvignon Blanc 1991   14   £C
Very Oz but also very not. You get the usual fruit but it's
unusually well polished and refined. Do they take Australians at Eton?

Mitchelton Wood-Matured Marsanne 1989   14   £D
Sticking wine in wood is often like sticking go faster stripes
on a car. The addition makes a fashionable difference and

it costs more. In this case, the difference is noticeable, so much so that carpenters will enjoy the well-polished result.

Mountarrow Reserve Chardonnay 1990   14   £C
I could do without the silly accredited landscape on the label but not without the glorious fruitscape in the bottle. Lovely wine.

AUSTRIAN WINE – *white*

Grüner Veltliner 1990   13   £C
An odd wine made from the eponymous grüner veltliner grape variety which is only grown, as far as I know, in Austria. It has a degree of engaging fruitiness and it's clean and respectable with it, but a curious bright, zesty quality lurks within it, rather like a sober civil servant who secretes floral underpants beneath his pinstripes. Well worth its rating though, as long as it doesn't go over the four-quid mark.

BULGARIAN WINE – *red*

Mavrud 1985, Assenovgrad   13   £B

Merlot/Gamza n.v.   13   £A

CHILEAN WINE – *red*

Concha y Toro, Cabernet Sauvignon 1989   13 £C
I've said of previous vintages of this wine that it was one to
put to the decanter test; shrouded in lead crystal twinkling
under candlelight, it will cozen many folk into thinking it
an arty-farty bordeaux of an ancient château. This '89 has
a little way to go before it can pass this test.

ENGLISH WINE – *white*

Hastings, Carr Taylor n.v.   14 £C
The first English wine I've enthused over: dry, woody,
edgily herby, with a good clean finish. Rather like an
Alsatian in some respects but without such a fruity bark.

FRENCH WINE – *red*

Bourgogne, Hautes-Côtes de Beaune 1989   13 £D

Cabernet Sauvignon, Vin de Pays d'Oc 1990   13 £C

Cahors, Côtes d'Olt 1989   13 £B

Château Bourdac 1988   11 £D

**Château d'Agassac 1986, Ludon
Haut-Médoc   13 £E**
Very dark colour. Nice soft, fruity nose. Pleasant, well-
balanced wine, very easy to drink.

Château de Nages 1990, Costières de Nîmes 13 £B
A warm, fruity soup of a wine which, though indistinct in
aroma, is firm and full in the taste department.

Château Grand-Puy-Lacoste 1987 13 £F
A famous old name best kept in a dark place for a while
before opening. Needs another five years to show itself off
at its lip-smackin' best, although it is impressive now.

Château Léoville-Barton 1987 14 £F
You owe it to yourself, sometimes, to enjoy a classic bordeaux, and this is one.

Château Marseau 1990 12 £B

Chorey-les-Beaune, Domaine Maillard 1989 14 £D
Deliciously light-style burgundy: true pinot character,
smell and taste. Could pass for a fancier wine from the
same area costing twice as much.

Claret, Patrice Calvet 1988 12 £C

Côte-Rôtie, Emile Champet 1986 15 £F
Gorgeous. Pricey, but still gorgeous, and we all deserve a
little fling occasionally. This wine is what the peasant
millionaire drinks, for it is totally down to earth yet hum-
ming with complex fruit and calm acid, friendly tannins,
and it is a superb fruit soup. That said, the wine will be
even better in ten years if stored correctly.

Côtes de Duras 1989, Seigneuret 12 £B

Côtes du Rhône 1990 (Waitrose) 13 £B

Côtes du Ventoux, Paul Boutinot 1990 15 £B
Monsieur Boutinot, venturing south from his beaujolais,
has made a splendid wine which is a great bargain for the
money since it comes across as a real southern Côtes du

Rhône of class and distinction. We even get that delicious
touch of pepper on the fruit – courtesy of the syrah grape,
perhaps.

**Crozes-Hermitages 1988, Cave des
Clairmonts**   12   £C

Dame Adelaide 1988   13   £C
Sounds like an Aussie drag queen, but is, in fact, a sober-
sided citizen with quite an aristocratic fruity dryness to it.

Domaine de Beauséjour 1989   11   £B

**Domaine de la Solitude, Châteauneuf-du-Pape
1989**   12   £D

**Domaine de St-Macaire, Vin de Pays de l'Herault
n.v.**   11   £A
Made by Baron de Rascas who, nominally at least, deserves encouragement. This wine needs more fruit to score
more than it does.

Domaine des Fontaines 1991   17   £B
Simply one of the most sublime merlots for the money I've
ever tasted. It is utterly caressingly soft and delicious and
so classy it is staggering.

**Domaine du Petit Clocher 1989, Anjou
Rouge**   12   £B

Domaine St-Germain 1990   13   £B

Gamay Haut-Poitou 1990   12   £B

**Good Ordinary Claret Bordeaux n.v.
(Waitrose)**   13   £B

Hautes Côtes de Beaune 1989   13   £C

Les Forts de Latour 1985, Pauillac   13   £G

Mâcon Supérieur, Caves de Lugny 1990   14   £C
A bargain red burgundy of some heft.

Margaux 1989   12   £E

Médoc 1990   12   £C

Moncenay 1989   11   £C

Moulin-à-Vent, Château de Chenas 1990   13   £C
Considering the outrageous prices of beaujolais crus nowadays, this is inexpensive. However, I'd cellar it for a couple
more years, maybe longer, until it repays its cost, and its
weight of alcohol and potential for development make it into
a minor red burgundy of greater complexity and class. That
said, the wine is perfectly drinkable now.

Moulins de Citran 1989 (half)   13   £C

**Nuits-St-Georges 1988, Caves des Hautes
Côtes**   10   £F
Scandalous price for a wine of no great shakes.

Pinot Noir d'Alsace 1990   12   £C

Pinot Noir d'Alsace, Cuvée Ancienne 1989   14   £D
This beguiling wine (rich and gamey, yet fresh and satiny)
is great, well chilled, with almost everything from fish to
pork sausages.

Prieuré de Fonclaire 1990   13   £B

Sarget de Gruaud Larose 1984, St-Julien   13   £E
A pungent, meaty bordeaux. Second wine of an efficient
vineyard which is always good but always a mite dull.

| Savigny-les-Beaune 1990, Faiveley | 13 | £E |

| Special Reserve Claret n.v. (Waitrose) | 13 | £C |

Properly developed fruit, attractive tannins and acidity. An approachable bordeaux.

| St-Amour 1991, Les Poulets | 12 | £C |

| St-Chinian n.v. | 11 | £A |

| St-Emilion n.v. | 13 | £C |

| St-Joseph, Caves de St-Désirat 1988 | 15 | £D |

Named after the patron saint of cuckolds, this wine is enough to make being cuckolded worth savouring – a glorious bottle of rich, dark wine which enters into a no-holds-barred wrestling match with the taste-buds. It floors the tongue with its soft, fruity richness and nervous, spicy edging neatly trimmed in velvet.

| Vieux Château Gaubert 1989 | 12 | £D |

FRENCH WINE – *white*

| Alsace Gewürztraminer 1990 | 12 | £C |

| Best de Bordeaux Tradition 1990 | 13 | £C |

Lots of creamy, woody undertones. Excellent with grilled chicken.

| Blanc de Mer n.v. | 16 | £B |

I groaned when I first saw this wine. That name! That label! The worst kind of abomination which the worst type of Côte d'Azur seafront café, overcharging the simple-minded tourist like mad, has fronting its house wine. The back label makes one suspicious, too, with its description of the wine as 'dry, fresh and crisp with an amazing depth and intensity of fruit flavour'. And who is this Pierre Guéry named on the label? And, lastly, where on earth is La Chapelle-Huelin, the site of his vineyard? But what do you know? (Or, rather, what do *I* know?) The wine is bloody marvellous stuff and absolutely glorious with all kinds of fish and tastes exactly like the back label says it does. Monsieur Guéry, you are a cunning genius – if you'd put muscadet on the label, as you could have done, I suspect, and charged us two and a half times the price, we'd all pass by on the other side of the street with our noses in the air. As it is, Waitrose, no less cunning than M. Guéry, are handing us one of the wine bargains of the year.

Blaye Blanc 1991 14 £B

A bargain fish wine. Balanced, dry yet nicely fruity, it leaves you wondering how you got away with spending so little.

Bordeaux Sauvignon 1991 12 £C

Bourgogne Aligote 1990, Brocard 13 £C

Not a bad wine – reminiscent of a sauvignon at its steely/fruity best.

Bourgogne Blanc 1990, Cave de Buxy 12 £C

Cabernet Rosé Haut-Poitou VDQS 1991 13 £B

Chablis 1990, Alain Couperot (half) 13 £C

Chablis 1990, Gaec des Réugnis 13 £D

Chablis Premier Cru, Beauroy 1990 13 £E

Flint and gunsmoke. No, not the Crimean War but a classic chablis.

Chais Beaumière Chardonnay 1990   14   £C
Excellent, rich chardonnay. Melony-bright with a dry,
clean finish.

Chardonnay Haut-Poitou 1991   13   £C

**Chardonnay, Vin de Pays du Jardin de la France
1990**   11   £C

**Château Bastor-Lamontagne 1988 and 1989,
Sauternes (half)**   13   £C
Useful half-bottle of dessert wine for small dinner parties:
rich, honeyed and ripe on the nose.

Château Darzac 1990   13   £C
A delicious balance of cleanness and fruitiness. Shellfish
will die for it.

Château de Rochemorin 1990   13   £D

Château la Calevie, Monbazillac 1989   14   £C
Happiness in a bottle – especially if drunk with hard fruit
pastries.

Château Loupiac Gaudiet 1988   13   £D
A pudding wine of character and richness – but best kept
for the Christmas pudding in the year 2000, at which time
it will mature into something even tastier and more
complex.

Château Piada 1989   13   £F

Château Septy 1987, Monbazillac   14   £C
A bouquet of spring flowers coated with honey and toffee
combines to produce a wine of richness that never sinks
into the cloying or heavy.

Clos Floridene 1990 13 £E

Finesse, elegance, fruitiness, acidity, dryness – all great mates for mackerel with mustard sauce – but if you're spending this much on a bottle of white wine you may feel mackerel is rather a comedown with it. Feel again.

Domaine de Grandchamp 1990 13 £C

Domaine de Hauret 1990 15 £C

Mouth-filling richness of fruit plus elegant acidity. It could only be a classic dry white graves, and so it is. Superb.

Domaine Petit Chateau Chardonnay 1990 13 £C

Ginestet Bordeaux Blanc n.v. 11 £C

Mâcon Lugny, Les Charmes 1990 13 £D

Menetou-Salon 1990 13 £D

Sancerre in all but name, but with a touch less gooseberry.

Meursault-Bouchères 1987 11 £G

Pinot Blanc d'Alsace 1991 14 £C

A very elegant dry wine which crustaceans blissfully die for.

Pouilly-Fuisse, Les Chevrières 1990 11 £E

Pouilly-Fumé, Jean-Claude Châtelain 1990 11 £E

Premières Côtes de Bordeaux n.v. 13 £B

A minor dessert wine. Toffee-apple freshness makes it too light for rich puds but fine with fresh, crisp fruits. Good price.

Sancerre, Manoir du Fort 1990 13 £D

Sauvignon Haut-Poitou 1991 13 £C

St-Véran 1990, Cellier des Samsons   12   £D

Tokay Pinot Gris 1990   12   £C

Trois Moulins Sauvignon 1991   14   £C
Farmyard pongs mingling with ripe melon fruit and lemon
zest. Very comforting drinking and very good value.

Vilonds Muscat 1991   12   £B

Vin de Pays d'Oc Sur Lie n.v.   14   £B
'Sur lie' by name but not surly by nature. 'Sur lie' simply
means that the wine has been allowed to acquire character
from its sediment (prior to filtering and bottling), and the
result is a lovely touch of southern fruitiness on the prim
acidity. Forget muscadet. This is half the price and twice
as good.

Vin de Savoie, Jacquère 1990   14   £C
A revelation: a delightful blend of soft fruit and acidity
which is floral and herby, yet clean. Buy it instead of
expensive white burgundies.

Vouvray, Domaine de la Robinière 1990   12   £C

GERMAN WINE – *white*

Avelsbacher Hammerstein Riesling 1983   15   £D
So intensely clean and lemonic that it can wash away a
whole day's cares in one mouthful drunk in the early
evening. At 7.5 per cent alcohol one cheerful and lucky
soul can polish off a whole bottle.

Bad Bergzaberner Kloster Liebfrauenberg
1990 15 £C
What a mouthful! What a bargain! Slap it on your taste-buds
and listen to 'em cry for more, more, more.

Baden Dry n.v. 13 £B
Good-value, fruity dry wine.

Niersteiner Dry 1989, Rheinhessen 11 £C

Oppenheimer Herrenberg Riesling Spätlese
1988, Rheinhessen 13 £D
Lovely aperitif. Delightfully controlled, soft fruitiness.

Riesling 1990 (Waitrose) (1 litre) 11 £B

Riesling Burg-Layer 1990 14 £C
Fabulous wine to have with cold meats and salads.

ITALIAN WINE – *red*

Campo ai Sassi 1989 14 £C
Delicious, rich, teeth-clinging dryness and fruitiness.

Cannonau del Parteolla 1990 (magnum) 13 £D

Carafe Red Wine (Waitrose) (1 litre) 13 £B
A highly drinkable wine for lots of pasta and lots of people.

Chianti Classico Riserva 1982, Montecastelli 12 £D
Good value if you revere older wine. It grabs the teeth like a
Rottweiler – and holds on with masses of veteran fruit.

Grifi 1987, Avignonesi 13 £F
A lot of money, but a lot of wine. Elegantly earthy and fruity.

Le Pergole Torte 1986, Monte Vertine   13   £G

Montepulciano d'Abruzzo 1990   15   £C
This is as irresistible to put to your lips after inhaling the
aroma as is the skin of a newly washed baby to its parent.
And as soft as a baby's bottom, too. Great, glorious,
glugging, soft fruity wine with so much happiness swirling
in the glass it restores your faith (like babies do).

Teroldego Rotaliano 1990   13   £C

ITALIAN WINE – *white*

Carafe White (Waitrose) (1 litre)   13   £B
Excellent value, very attractive, well-balanced dry white.

Chardonnay Alto Adige, Walch 1990   15   £C
One of the best and most elegant chardonnays made in
Northern Italy.

Il Marzocco, Chardonnay 1988   13   £F
It is stylish, clear and fresh, with an almost exotic Italian
spiciness to the typical chardonnay aroma and taste.

Orvieto Classico, Cardeto 1991   11   £C

Santa Cristina Chardonnay 1989, Zenato   14   £D
Lovely aperitif chardonnay with a delicious acid/fruit
aroma.

Soave Classico, Zenato 1991   14   £C
I never get to taste better soaves than Signor Zenato's.

Tocai di San Martino della Battaglia 1990,
Zenato   13   £C

LEBANESE WINE – *red*

Château Musar 1983 and 1985	16 '83	£D
	14 '85	£D

I used to say of this wine that it was the greatest wine made for a fiver under fire. The fire has gone, thank God, and, alas, so has the fiver. But the wine is still a tremendous, spicy, volatile beast, though the later vintages don't seem so complex or vivid.

NEW ZEALAND WINE – *red*

Cook's Hawkes Bay Cabernet Sauvignon 1987	11	£C
Savidge Estate Cabernet/Merlot 1989	12	£C

NEW ZEALAND WINE – *white*

Cook's Chardonnay 1991	12	£C
Villa Maria Sauvignon Blanc 1991	14	£C

This is like an unusually fruity and assertive sancerre. It is excellent drinking and better value than almost all sancerres on sale.

PORTUGUESE WINE – *red*

Bairrada Reserva 1987, Dom Ferraz   14   £B
Outstanding value for a fruity wine of such versatility: it
can be savoured by itself (light enough), accompany main
courses (its open, fruity style is good with food), and it has
enough acidity to cope with cheeses.

Pasmados 1986   13   £C

Tinto da Anfora 1988   14   £C
Sticky toffee-and-fig aroma, ripe rich fruit and a nice
finish.

SOUTH AFRICAN WINE – *red*

Far Enough 1991   14   £B
I've always – and I admit the prejudice freely – been
pleased when so many South African wines failed to tickle
my fancy because that country's politics so sickened me.
This wine is difficult to dislike, however, for it is truly a
superb little bargain. Clos de Vougeot it ain't, but it's a
decent, fruity pinot noir which is eminently gulpable, and
good chilled.

Stellenryck Cabernet Sauvignon 1987   13   £D

SOUTH AFRICAN WINE – *white*

Avontuur Chardonnay 1991	12	£C
Sauvignon Blanc KWV 1991	12	£C
Stellenryck Chardonnay 1990	12	£C

SPANISH WINE – *red*

Agramont Navarra 1989   15   £C
Fabulous blend of tempranillo and cabernet sauvignon. Delicious concentration of fruit – dry, lengthy, distinguished.

Castillo de Liria Valencia n.v.   15   £A
Superb value. A simple, soft, fruity wine of no great complexity but toothsome drinkability. Ripe blackcurrant on the nose, cherries on the palate and a mix of the two in the throat.

Cosme Palacio Rioja 1988	13	£C
Don Hugo n.v.	13	£B
Ribera del Duero 1989	13	£C
Viña Alberdi Rioja 1987	13	£D

SPANISH WINE – *white*

Castillo de Liria Valencia (magnum)	14	£C

Conde de Caralt 1989   13   £B
Dry, elegant, very good value – like a Peter Ustinov
anecdote.

Cune Rioja Blanco Seco Reserva 1985   10   £D

USA WINE – *red*

Barrow Green Pinot Noir 1987, California   15   £E
A little beauty – hums with vegetal, calm fruit. Much like a
good volnay and excellent value at the price.

Cartlidge & Browne, Zinfandel 1990   14   £C
Zingy, zesty stuff which just flows down the throat and
screams with fruitiness all through the descent. Not as lush
as the '89 vintage.

Mountain View Pinot Noir 1989   13   £C

Wente Cabernet Sauvignon 1987   12   £D

USA WINE – *white*

St Andrew's Vineyard Chardonnay 1990   12   £E

YUGOSLAVIAN WINE – *red*

Milion Merlot 1988   13   £A

Milion Pinot Noir 1988   12   £A

SPARKLING WINE/CHAMPAGNE

Angas Brut Rosé n.v. Australian   14   £C
Good stuff at heart. And at under a fiver, a good thing to take to formal dinner parties.

Blanquette de Limoux n.v. (Waitrose)   12   £D

Cava Cristal Brut Castellblanch, Spain n.v.   11   £D

Champagne n.v. (Waitrose)   15   £F
Superb, quite superb for the money. A rich, dry wine, which froths beautifully.

Champagne 1986 (Waitrose)   14   £G
Gee, a lot of money. But if you must drink vintage champagne, this one is outstanding.

Champagne Rosé n.v. (Waitrose)   15   £F
Biscuity edge to the fruit, which is perfectly developed. A lovely rosé.

Comtesse de Die Tradition 1990   14   £D
Wonderful peachy aperitif. Delicious, appetite-arousing stuff.

Crémant de Bourgogne, Blanc de Noirs n.v.   14   £D
Excellent balanced wine from black grapes: rich, dry, classy. A bargain. You could serve it at a royal wedding.

Crémant de Bourgogne, Lugny n.v.   14   £D
Excellent dry (yet fruitily rounded) sparkling wine, to be preferred to many, many champagnes.

Crémant de Bourgogne, Sparkling Rosé n.v.   13   £D

Extra Dry Non-Vintage Champagne n.v.
(Waitrose)   12   £F

Extra Dry Vintage Champagne 1983
(Waitrose)   17   £G
An absolutely glorious light champagne of perfumed
elegance and beauty – it celebrates itself. Quite delicious –
a bubbly of such forward and forthright charm that even
novices say, 'My word, this is something special, isn't it?' I
think it has to do with hollyhocks – how did they charm
their faintly aromatic way into the wine?

Le Baron de Beaumont Chardonnay n.v.   14   £C
Excellent value for a delightful little sparkler.

Moscato d'Asti 1990   15   £C
This is the wine I'd hand around to the firing squad before
they shot me. They could finish me off while I finished a
glass and I'd die happy. It is a semi-sparkler and it is
medium-sweet, but there is little semi or medium about it
in truth, for it is a full-blown pudding wine or – a large
glass only – an amusing aperitif.

Santi Chardonnay Brut n.v.   14   £C
Under a fiver? Snap it up!

Saumur n.v. (Waitrose)   14   £D
Chewy little number of some distinction.

Sparkling Liebfraumilch n.v. (Waitrose)   13   £C
Great fizzy, fruity fun for the parents/teachers get-
togethers.